E
JCES:
Planning
Career

ham and Sandy Stryker
eene, Penelope Paine
and Kathleen Peters
Production coordinated by Christine Nolt
Illustrated by Itoko Maeno, Janice Blair,
Alma Barkley, Dorie Hutchinson
and Laurie Whitfield

Advocacy Press, Santa Barbara, California

 To Wendy and Bill

Copies of this book may be ordered by sending $17.45 ppd. to *More Choices,* Advocacy Press, P.O. Box 236, Dept. A, Santa Barbara, CA 93102. (California residents add sales tax.)

Proceeds from the sale of this book will benefit the Girls Club of Santa Barbara, Inc. and contribute to the further development of programs for girls and young women aged 6 to 18.

Copyright © 1987 by Melinda Bingham and Sandra Stryker
Revised 1988
Library of Congress Card No. 87-11494

ISBN 0-911655-28-X

All rights reserved. No part of this book may be reproduced in any form without permission in writing from Advocacy Press, P.O. Box 236, Santa Barbara, California 93102, except by a newspaper or magazine reviewer who wishes to quote brief passages in a review.

 Published by Advocacy Press, P.O. Box 236, 531 East Ortega Street, Santa Barbara, California 93103, a subsidiary of the the Girls Club of Santa Barbara

Printed in the United States of America

10 9 8 7 6 5 4 3 2

Contents

Introduction		4
Chapter one	The Myths...	7
Chapter two	...Versus the Realities	25
Chapter three	Money: How Important Is It?	41
Chapter four	A Parent's Limited Resources: Time, Money and Energy	63
Chapter five	Career Planning for Flexibility and Higher Salary	79
Chapter six	Why Do We Choose What We Choose?	105
Chapter seven	Skills and Attitudes that Will Give You Control	125
Chapter eight	Keeping Your Life in Balance	155
Chapter nine	Managing Your Relationships	173
Chapter ten	Children and Child Care: Careful Planning Pays Off	191
Chapter eleven	Your Own Strategic Plan For Mixing Career and Family	203
Chapter twelve	Better Choices for Future Generations	219
Index & Contributors		238
Notes		239

Introduction

Only a few years ago, millions of American women were confidently declaring that, "I can have it all." The results included many valiant efforts, a few glorious successes—and too many failures and frustrations. Today, the call is more likely to be a disheartened, "I've had enough."

Mixing career and family life, it seems, is not as easy as we once thought. But, like it or not, there is no turning back. Social and financial pressures keep most women in the workforce even when their children are very young. Millions of women are their family's sole support. Most women who work outside the home are also responsible for the great majority of household and child care tasks. For too many American families today, poverty is all too real, stress is ever-present and there is never enough time. Yet most people still use the "Ozzie and Harriet"/"Father Knows Best" approach to career and life planning, as though there are no single parents, poverty and stress; as though most women don't really need to work and there is no connection between career and family life.

More Choices is based on the theory that career and family planning are intrinsically related, and therefore must be approached as a unit. Higher paying jobs allow a parent to work fewer hours, have more flexibility, and more time for raising a family.

In our work, we see that women still have unrealistic expectations for their lives. On the one extreme, they express attitudes such as:

> *"Since marriage and motherhood are my main goals in life, there's no need for me to take my education seriously. It would just be a waste of money, time and energy to prepare for a career."*

> *"I 'might' have a job sometime, but my income will be supplemental. I'll never need a career that could support my family."*

> *"It's enough responsibility for me to be in charge of things at home. If I need to have an outside job, I only have enough energy to work in a supportive role. I don't want to be the boss."*

Then there's the opposite extreme:

> *"I can have it all and do it all—perfectly. Who says you can't get by on four hours of sleep a night?"*

> *"My career takes so much time and energy I'm afraid I have little choice but to abandon my hopes for a family."*

This book is intended to address the problems of the real world, the one we all live in now, like it or not. It is meant to be a career-planning guide for young people and a life-planning tool for adults. Anyone contemplating or attempting to balance career and family life should find it helpful. Although the characters in most of the examples are women, the exercises are designed to be used by readers of either sex. Men, too, will find this process enlightening.

More Choices builds on the skills first outlined in earlier books. Readers who would like to learn more about values clarification, budgeting, decision making, goal setting, assertiveness, skills identification and career planning may wish to consult CHOICES: *A Teen Woman's Journal for Self-awareness and Personal Planning*, CHALLENGES: *A Young Man's Journal for Self-awareness and Personal Planning* or CHANGES: *A Woman's Journal for Self-awareness and Personal Planning*.

It is our hope that everyone who works through this book will come away with greater awareness of life's problems and possibilities, improved self-knowledge and the beginning of a plan for a balanced and fulfilling life. The problems and needs of American families are so compelling that, ultimately, society will have to change to accommodate them. We hope that *More Choices* will provide some interim answers, and be a workable tool for the duration.

"One cannot collect all the beautiful shells on the beach."

Anne Morrow Lindbergh

CHAPTER ONE
The Myths...

The happy do not believe in miracles.
—Johann W. von Goethe

Nothing is more difficult than
competing with a myth.
—Francoise Giroud

Emma Neezer-Scrooge couldn't sleep, though it was late and she was certainly tired enough. Her day had been rough, but typical. She'd been up at 5 a.m. to get in a half hour of aerobics before the kids woke up. She made breakfast for them and her husband, Tim; cleaned the house; threw a load of clothes in the washer; put on her best skirt and jacket; and was only ten minutes late for the breakfast meeting downtown. Then there were the usual problems at the office, an important board meeting of the United Way, and a report that her boss, Roberta Cratchit, said absolutely had to be completed by the end of the day. The end of the day turned out to be 9 p.m., but Emma often worked later than that. By the time she got home, Tim was furious. "What's more important to you," he demanded to know, "your job or your family?"

Emma promised once again to try to make more time for her family responsibilities, but she didn't see how she could possibly do it all. "How did I ever get into this situation?" she wondered as she finally drifted off to sleep at 2 a.m.

"What's that?" a startled Emma cried as she sat up in bed. She distinctly heard the rattling of pots and pans and the creaking of station wagon doors. Suddenly, a human-like form appeared. "Who are you? What do you want?" Emma demanded. "Oh, I hope I didn't frighten you, dear. Could I get you a glass of milk or something? How about a nice sandwich? I know you didn't take time to eat a proper dinner. You're sure you don't want anything? Well, then, let me introduce myself. I am the Ghost of Women's Past. Your dear Grandmother Marley asked me and two other spirits to stop by tonight and explain the myths."

"What myths?" asked Emma. "Just follow me, dear," the ghost replied. "And do put on your robe. I wouldn't want you to catch a chill."

Emma suddenly found herself transported from her home and surrounded by a heavy fog. Periodically, visions and sounds would fade in and out as the Ghost of Women's Past stood quietly and pointed to the ever-changing parade of images. The first delegation of women, Emma thought, could have been created by Walt Disney. Emma saw Cinderella, Sleeping Beauty and Snow White walking arm-in-arm as they sang a sad, slow version of "Some Day My Prince Will Come." Behind them marched several generations of "sex symbols," including Mae West, Jean Harlow, Marilyn Monroe and Jane Mansfield. They, too, had vacant, unhappy expressions. Then came the Blue Ribbon Panel of TV Moms, led by Harriet Nelson, June Cleaver, Margaret Anderson and Laura Petrie. They could not have looked more dejected if they had just been drummed out of the PTA.

"What's wrong with them? Why do they look so unhappy?" Emma wanted to know. "They all made the same mistake," the spirit said. "They accepted the myths. They thought there would always be someone around to take care of them, or that it was more important to be pleasing to others than to please themselves. They thought motherhood would take up their entire lives and, now that the kids are grown, they aren't sure what they should be doing. They let someone else write the scripts for their lives. They never really existed."

"That's what **I** was going to say," Emma replied. "If you're supposed to be the Ghost of Women's Past, where are all the **real** women? Where are the black women, the Orientals and the Hispanics? Where are the working moms and the poor women?"

"I guess the people who created the myths didn't want to complicate things with the truth. And the results weren't good for anyone. While one group of women was frustrated trying to live up to an unhealthy ideal, the others were left feeling excluded and unacceptable. Be careful, dear. The myths are fading, but they are still out there." At this, the Ghost of Women's Past disappeared. She was soon replaced by a rather exhausted-looking spirit with a briefcase in one hand and a bag of groceries in the other.

"Sorry I'm a little late," she apologized. "I got hung up with another client. You know how it is. You're Emma, right? I'm the Ghost of Women's Present. Is it okay with you if we get right to work here? I have one more appointment; then I have to pick up the dog at the vet's and my in-laws are coming for dinner, so I don't have much time for small talk."

Before Emma could reply, she found herself in what appeared to be a factory. A treadmill stretched out before her as far as she could see. On the treadmill, thousands of women were running—or at least moving their feet. As far as Emma could tell, they weren't getting very far. Emma heard bits of conversation echoing through the vast space of the factory: "running late"…"maybe next week"…"pencil me in" … "sorry I'm late"…"have to check with the sitter"…"I'll have the report tomorrow"…"I know I promised, but"…"are you sure you can't get someone else to do it?"…"just give me five more minutes"…"is it really that late?"

"Goodness," Emma exclaimed. "What's going on here?"

"These are the models for the new myth. They're supposed to be able to do everything perfectly and all at once. Unfortunately, some of the kinks haven't been worked out yet. Every time they add a new function to their programming, a few more models break down. I never noticed before, but they look a bit like you and me, don't they?"

"Maybe," Emma agreed. "At least they don't look as sad as the old models."

"Well, I think maybe they're too exhausted to look sad. Listen, I have to run. You take care, now." With that, the ghost nearly vanished, then reappeared. "Sorry, almost forgot my keys. You don't see a laundry ticket around here anywhere, do you? Here it is. Well, bye!"

The third spirit then appeared, a much calmer version, Emma thought. "You've probably figured out that I'm the Ghost of Women's Future," the apparition said. "Or at least I could be. Would you like to take a look?"

This time, Emma liked what she saw. There were men and women working together as equals and sharing family responsibilities. Emma saw happy families and well-cared-for children. Everyone, in fact, seemed healthier and more satisfied with their lives. "That's what I want," cried Emma. "That's what I've wanted all the time. Why don't I have it and how can I get it?"

"First we have to break away from the myths," the spirit said. "The old ones **and** the new ones. The myths of the past put so many limitations on women that it's not surprising they were replaced with the myth that there are no limitations at all. But no one can live in a myth.

"What we need to do now is **plan.** We need to plan our own lives so that they hold as much personal and career satisfaction as possible. And then we need to plan for a society that will make things easier for the next generation. It's a big task, but it promises to be a rewarding one. Are you up for it, Emma?"

"Up?" Emma murmured, opening her eyes to find Tim standing over her.

"Better get up, Em," he said, handing her a cup of hot coffee as a peace offering. "You've got a big day ahead."

"Yes," Emma said. "I think it's about time I got started."

As Emma discovered, it's necessary to look at the past before you can look to the future. For women, the past was populated with myths about who they were and what they could do. The rules change from time to time, but one thing is consistently true: Myths don't hold up well under examination. Let's take a closer look at some of the most prevalent tales.

11

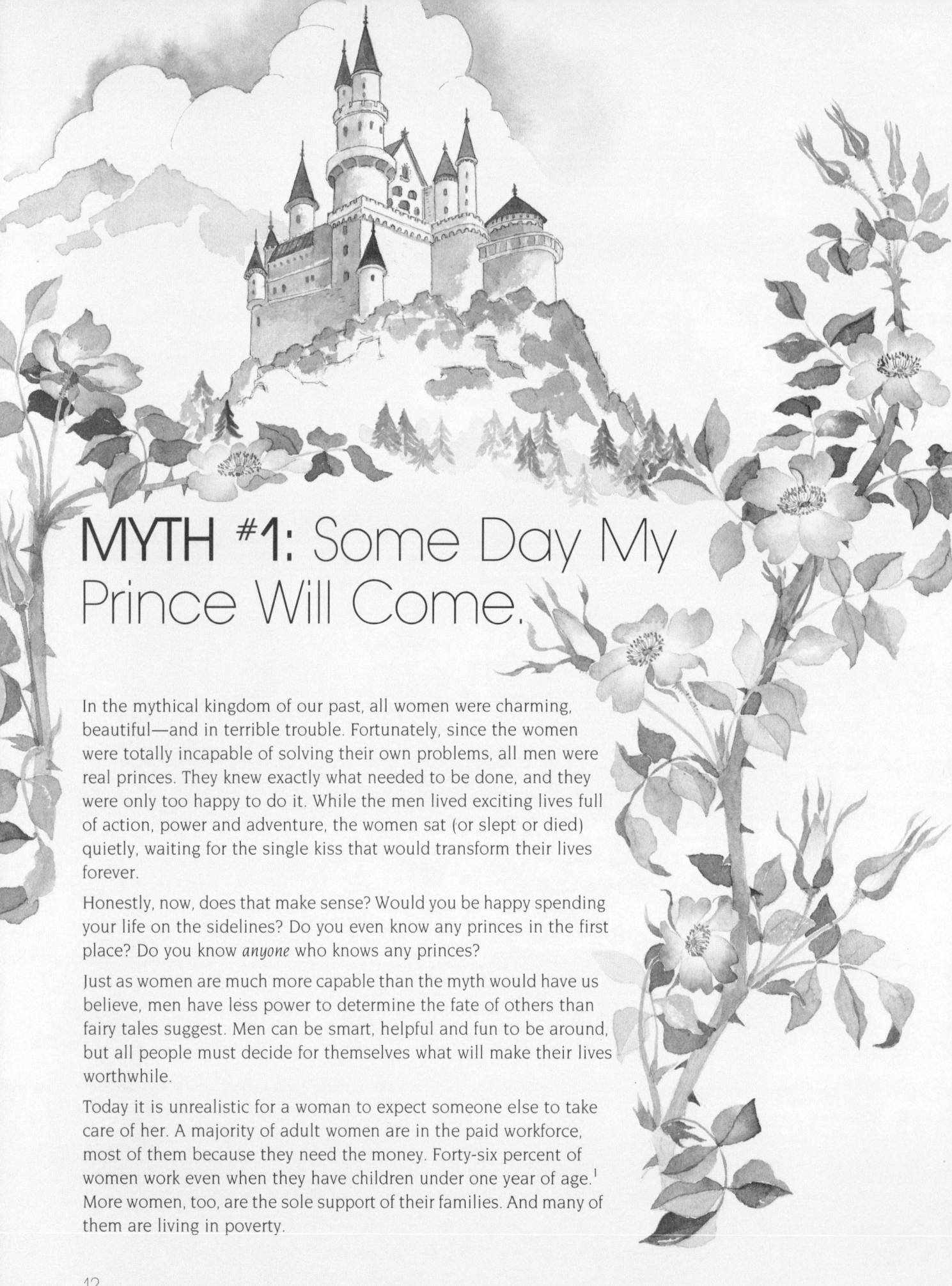

MYTH #1: Some Day My Prince Will Come.

In the mythical kingdom of our past, all women were charming, beautiful—and in terrible trouble. Fortunately, since the women were totally incapable of solving their own problems, all men were real princes. They knew exactly what needed to be done, and they were only too happy to do it. While the men lived exciting lives full of action, power and adventure, the women sat (or slept or died) quietly, waiting for the single kiss that would transform their lives forever.

Honestly, now, does that make sense? Would you be happy spending your life on the sidelines? Do you even know any princes in the first place? Do you know *anyone* who knows any princes?

Just as women are much more capable than the myth would have us believe, men have less power to determine the fate of others than fairy tales suggest. Men can be smart, helpful and fun to be around, but all people must decide for themselves what will make their lives worthwhile.

Today it is unrealistic for a woman to expect someone else to take care of her. A majority of adult women are in the paid workforce, most of them because they need the money. Forty-six percent of women work even when they have children under one year of age.[1] More women, too, are the sole support of their families. And many of them are living in poverty.

New living patterns are beginning to emerge as society adjusts. Author John Naisbitt anticipated this in his book, *Megatrends*, when he said, "We experience change when there is a confluence of changing values and economic necessity."[2]

Today, in addition to the "traditional" family in which the husband holds an outside job while the wife stays home with the kids, we see:

> The two-career family with both partners earning salaries.
>
> The single professional devoting full-time to his or her career.
>
> The single parent supporting one or more children alone.
>
> The working wife with a husband who cares for the home or works only part-time.
>
> The cooperative living arrangement, in which two or more single parents and their children live together and share responsibility for childcare, household chores, and expenses.
>
> The working husband with a wife who works part-time and cares for the children.
>
> The blended family with children from one or more marriages living together with parents and step-parents.

There are many possibilities for achieving a satisfying lifestyle if you do two things:

1. Believe that at some time you are going to have to support yourself and, possibly, your family.

2. Keep your options open. Develop a plan for taking care of yourself and follow it through.

MYTH #2: It's Only a Story; No One Believes It.

As children, many of us heard the same stories over and over again. How much do these nursery rhymes and fairy tales affect our present beliefs?

They affect them more than you might think. The more often you hear something, the more likely you are to remember it. And, on a subconscious level at least, you begin to believe it. After awhile, you will even start repeating the message to yourself. And the tapes that run in your mind will begin to affect your conscious actions.

Consider our old friend, the prince, for example. He trotted through many of the fairy tales we heard as children. If you were to ask adult women if they believe in him, they would almost certainly deny it. Their actions, however, might lead you to believe otherwise. Millions of women have not prepared themselves to be self-supporting, presumably because they expect someone else to come along (preferably in a classy car rather than on a white charger) to take care of them.

The phrases below are examples of some of the messages related by many children's stories. Draw a line from the message or myth in the left column to the appropriate source in the right column. There may be more than one source for each message.

MESSAGES

Some day my prince will come.

And they lived happily ever after.

Women are vain and jealous.

Step-parents are evil.

Women belong in castles and towers.

Men belong on thrones or horses.

Women get what they want through magic, scheming or being "nice."

Men get what they want through work and bravery.

Women must have long hair and small feet.

Women need to be rescued.

Men are the rescuers.

Women are self-sacrificing.

Men go after what they want.

It's dangerous for girls to have adventures.

SOURCES

Cinderella

Snow White

Rapunzel

Sleeping Beauty

Hansel and Gretel

Beauty and the Beast

Little Red Riding Hood

Goldilocks and the Three Bears

Can you think of other messages? Other sources? _____

_____

_____

_____

_____

An Exception Worth Noting

Not *all* of the stories you heard as a child send negative messages. A few have important truths to deliver. Remember the ant and the grasshopper, for example? The grasshopper wiled away the summer playing her fiddle and scoffing at the ant, who worked hard in preparation for the winter. And when the winter came...well, we don't have to tell you who was laughing then. The ant was self-sufficient. That is, she could take care of herself. Her life may sound dreary, but that's because—until recently—the important second half of the fable was lost.

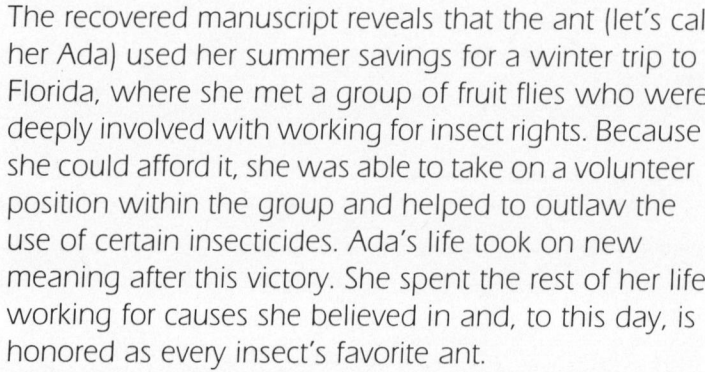

> The recovered manuscript reveals that the ant (let's call her Ada) used her summer savings for a winter trip to Florida, where she met a group of fruit flies who were deeply involved with working for insect rights. Because she could afford it, she was able to take on a volunteer position within the group and helped to outlaw the use of certain insecticides. Ada's life took on new meaning after this victory. She spent the rest of her life working for causes she believed in and, to this day, is honored as every insect's favorite ant.
>
> The grasshopper (Prudence) was less fortunate. Because she always depended on others to take care of her, she spent most of her time trying to be pleasing. For awhile she was attractive and amusing, and some of the most socially acceptable insects were happy to associate with her. As she got older, though, her popularity declined. She died alone, regretting most of all that she had squandered her life so freely.

Self-sufficiency made the difference. At first glance, you may have thought that Ada's self-sufficiency kept her from having an interesting and useful life. But the reverse is true. Because she could take care of herself, Ada was free to be the ant she wanted to be and to do as she pleased. Prudence's dependency, however, left her with no control over her life. She always had to try to please others. But she didn't know how to please herself, and no one had to try to please her.

TV Trivia

What do the popular TV shows of the past three decades have to say about sex roles and expectations? Since most popular programs have been widely syndicated for years, you are probably familiar with them, even if they are older than you are. Some are repeated often enough to be thought of as modern fairy tales. What have you learned from them? If you can't answer some of the questions—Good! Those messages have passed you by. If you don't watch TV and never have, you may skip this exercise.

1950s

In **I Love Lucy:** What is Ricky Ricardo's job? _____
What is Lucy Ricardo's job? _____

In **Father Knows Best:** What is Jim Anderson's job? _____
What is Margaret Anderson's job? _____

In **Perry Mason:** What does Perry Mason do? _____
What does Della Street do? _____
Is Della Street married? _____

In **Leave It To Beaver:** What does Ward Cleaver do? _____
What does June Cleaver do? _____

In **Our Miss Brooks:** What is Miss Brooks' job? _____
Is she married? _____
Does she want to get married? _____

In **How to Marry a Millionaire:** Are the main characters men or women? _____
What is their main ambition in life? _____

1960s

In **The Dick Van Dyke Show:** What is Rob Petrie's job? _____
What is Laura Petrie's job? _____
What is Sally Roger's job? _____
Is she married? _____
Would she like to be? _____

Is **Dr. Kildare:** A man or a woman? _____

In **Route 66:** Are the main characters men or women? _____
What do they do? _____

In **My Three Sons:** Is the single parent a man or a woman? _____

In **Gidget:** Is the single parent a man or a woman? _____

In **Bachelor Father:** Is the single parent a man or a woman? _____

17

In **Bonanza**: Is the single parent a man or a woman? _____

In **Star Trek**: What is Jim Kirk's job? _____

What is Mr. Spock's job? _____

What is Scott's job? _____

What is Bones' job? _____

What is Uhura's job? _____

1970s

In **The Mary Tyler Moore Show**: What is Mary Richards' job? _____

Is she married? _____

What is Lou Grant's job? _____

Is he married? _____

Does he have children? _____

In **All in the Family**: What is Archie Bunker's job? _____

What is Edith Bunker's job? _____

In **The Jeffersons**: What is George Jefferson's job? _____

What is Louise Jefferson's job? _____

In **M*A*S*H**: What is Hawkeye Pierce's job? _____

What is B.J. Hunnicut's job? _____

What is Margaret Hoolihan's job? _____

1980s

In **Hill Street Blues**: What is Lucy Bates' job? _____

Is she married? _____

What is Frank Furillo's job? _____

Is he married? _____

Does he have children? _____

What is Joyce Davenport's job? _____

Is she married? _____

Does she have children? _____

In **Miami Vice**: What do the main characters do? _____

Are they men or women? _____

In **Moonlighting**: What is Maddie Hayes' job? _____

What is David Addison's job? _____

In **Kate & Allie**: Are the single parents men or women? _____

In **The Cosby Show**: What does Cliff Huxtable do? _____

What does Claire Huxtable do? _____

Are they married? _____

Do they have children? _____

In **Family Ties**: What does Steven Keaton do? _____

What does Elyse Keaton do? _____

Where does she do her work? _____

Are they married? _____

Do they have children? _____

What messages do these TV shows send about the kinds of work men should do? _____
_____

What messages do these TV shows send about the kinds of work women should do? _____
_____

When men and women work together in these programs, who is usually the boss? _____
_____

If a woman works outside the home, is she more likely to be single or married? _____
_____

Do male TV characters often combine career, marriage and children? _____
_____

Do female TV characters often combine career, marriage and children? _____
_____

Are there many images of black, Asian, Hispanic or Native American women at home or at work?
_____

What changes do you see in the most recent TV shows? _____
_____

How accurately do the programs we've discussed represent the lives of women you know?
_____

MYTH #3: Motherhood is a Lifetime Job.

Phoebe was just four the first time someone asked her what she wanted to be when she grew up. "A mommy," Phoebe replied enthusiastically. As a child, Phoebe found taking care of her dolls to be a full-time job. Of course, Phoebe's "babies" were never toilet-trained. They never learned to feed themselves. They never went off to school without her. It never occurred to Phoebe that real children do all of those things. She married Vince as soon as she finished high school. They had two children, Mark and Alex, by the time she was twenty-one. Phoebe and Vince decided they couldn't afford a larger family, since both agreed it was important for Phoebe to stay home with the kids. By the time Phoebe was twenty-eight, both children were in school all day. She was just thirty-nine when Alex went away to college. When she considered that she might easily have forty more years ahead of her, she decided to get a job. With no training or work experience, she didn't earn much, but she liked being able to help with Mark's and Alex's college expenses. When they graduated, Phoebe decided to go to college herself. Some people teased her about going back to school at her age. But Phoebe laughed off their remarks. She had discovered that life offers more choices than she once thought.

Like Phoebe, most women want to be mothers. Statistics show that about 90% of American women eventually have children.[3] But there is a difference between being a **parent** and **parenting**. Times have changed since the '50s and early '60s, when motherhood was considered a lifetime job, for those who could afford it. At that time, the economy was booming, millions of people were moving from central cities into the suburbs, and couples were rearing large families. Men prided themselves on their earning capacity, and the fact that their wives didn't "have to" work outside the home. They often worked long hours and, with commuting time added to their workday, left their wives almost solely responsible for child care and housework.

For middle- and upper-class families, motherhood was a "calling." Besides the usual tasks related to taking care of a large house and four to six children, women devoted hours to the emotional, intellectual and social development of their children. Even then, though, housewives began to want something more from their lives. In 1963, Betty Friedan wrote a book called *The Feminine Mystique*, and ideas about women's roles began to change rapidly.

For many people, of course, the "cult of motherhood" was never a reality. Like the myths presented by the Ghost of Women's Past, the suburban Utopia was a prison for the minority of women who could buy into it, and a fantasy for the majority who lived a less affluent life.

Economics also helped to bring about changes in family life. As the economy slowed down in the early '70s, it became difficult for a family to live on one income alone, and millions of women entered or re-entered the workforce. Couples began to have smaller families, as well. Today, if you have children, you are more likely to have one or two children than you are to have four or five.

For all of these reasons, parenting is not likely to be your sole calling in life, though it may well be your most rewarding. How much time will child care take? Ask yourself the following questions to help visualize your life. *Start with the question at the bottom.* Draw a line from the question to the point on the graph which corresponds to your answer.

What age will you be when your last child graduates from high school?

Mark your age when your last child enters high school.

Mark your age when your last child enters junior high.

What age will you be when your last child enters kindergarten?

At what age do you expect to have your last child?

At what age do you expect to have your first child?

Now complete the following statements.

From the time I am _____ until I am _____ years old, child care could take a high percentage of my time. That equals a total of _____ years.

The most time-consuming aspects of child care should be completed by the time I am _____ years old.

By the time I am _____ years old, my children will have left home.

If I live to be 76, the average life expectancy for women, I will have _____ years to fill with commitments other than parenting.

MYTH #4: I Can Be a Superwoman.

The latest, and perhaps the cruelest, myth is the one that Emma Neezer-Scrooge bought into: the myth of the Superwoman. According to this myth, it is possible—it is even *expected*—that a woman do everything, and do it exceptionally well. A Superwoman should:

- Have a high-paid, high-pressure, full-time career—and excel at it.
- Have a good marriage to a successful, supportive man (who doesn't have to help out around the house).
- Take full responsibility for her children, who are always intelligent, clean, respectful, creative, and physically and emotionally healthy.
- Keep her home in perfect order.
- Be available for friends and family members at any time.
- Take part in community activities—preferably a leading part.
- Entertain lavishly and often.
- Take part in a sport, like running marathons or bike racing.
- Always be well dressed and perfectly groomed.
- Never get sick or tired.
- Remember the first name, birthday, and astrological sign of everyone she's ever met.

And those are just the basic requirements! Well, it can't be done. There isn't time. And no one excels at *everything*. Women who try to live by this myth find that, sooner or later, something has to go. They are constantly exhausted and may develop serious health problems.

Do you know anyone who is trying to live the Superwoman myth? Describe her life below.

What are her family responsibilities? _____

_____

If she works, what is her job? _____

What is a typical workday like for this woman? _____

_____

How much money does she earn? _____

How does she use her spare time? _____

_____

What help does she have with housework and other home chores? _____

We can do many things—maybe more than we think we can. But we need to decide what is most important to us, and do that first. This is called setting priorities. We also need to know how to say no, or to ask for help when we need it. Finally, it is essential to give ourselves enough time to relax, to recover, and to remember who we are and what it is we want to do with our lives. See Chapters 9 and 10 for more information on these topics.

MYTH #5: And They Lived Happily Ever After.

It's a good way to end a story. The people who used it probably thought repeating it often enough would make it true. Or perhaps they decided you really didn't have to know about Cinderella's divorce or Snow White's financial problems or Prince Charming's unemployment. But we aren't going to take the easy way out, and neither are you. We've devoted the next chapter to some unsettling truths about the lives of women today. Read on.

REFLECTIONS

In search of my mother's garden I
found my own.
—Alice Walker

CHAPTER TWO

...Versus the Realities

It is easier to believe a lie that one has
heard a thousand times than a fact
no one ever heard before.

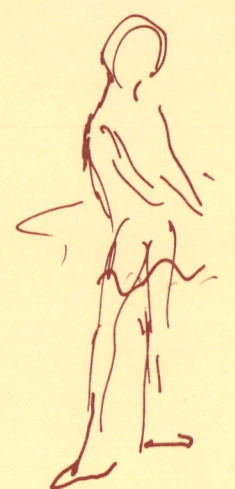
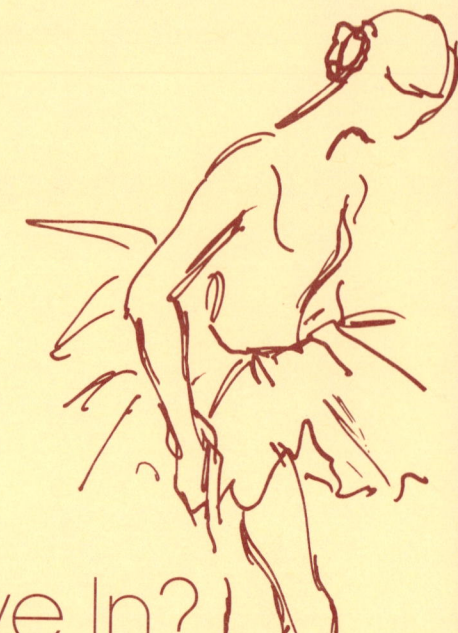

Which World Do You Live In?

A mythical world is an exciting place to live. It's pleasant to believe in its existence, even when the evidence around you indicates that the truth is something quite different. Before we talk about the real world in general, let's take a look at *your* world. Does it bear much resemblance to the myths of Chapter 1?

Put your name at the top of the list and then write the names of nine friends of any age.

Name	A	B	C	D	E	F	G	H	I	J
1.										
2.										
3.										
4.										
5.										
6.										
7.										
8.										
9.										
10.										

Now answer the following questions. If the questions below apply to any of the names above, put a check in the appropriate box.

In box A: **check** the people who live in a home where the man has a job outside the home and the woman is a full-time homemaker.

In box B: **check** the people who are divorced or, if living with their parents, the parents are divorced.

In box C: **check** the people living in a single-parent household.

In box D: **check** if that single-parent household is headed by a woman.

In box E: **write the number of children** living in each household.

In box F: place a **P** if the mothers in that home work part-time or an **F** if they work full-time.

In box G: place a **check** if there are children in that home who are in grade school or high school.

In box H: place a **check** if there are children in that home under the age of 6.

In box I: **write the job title** for those women who work outside the home.

In box J: write a **C** if you think the family could live comfortably on the mother's income, and an **NC** if you don't think they could. If you are not sure, you might look up the average salary for that job in your local classified ads or ask someone who might know what that type of job would pay.

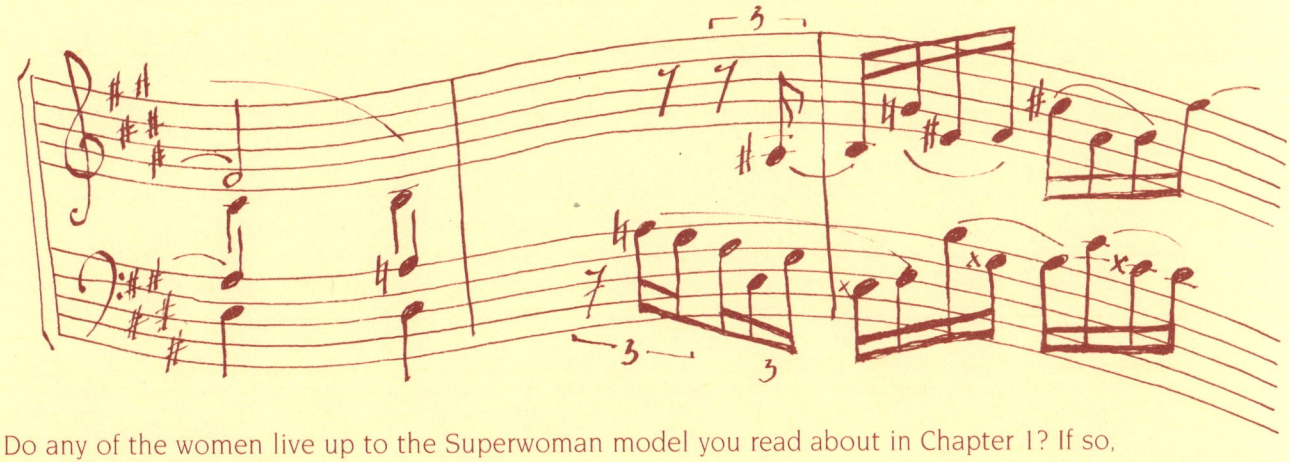

Do any of the women live up to the Superwoman model you read about in Chapter 1? If so, describe her life below.

_____
_____
_____
_____
_____

Use the information you've gathered to summarize the facts about women in your world. Fill in the blanks with statistics from your chart.

In _____'s world, the "traditional" family with the man
      your name

working and the woman at home exists for _____ % (number you found × 10) of

those polled. _____ % are divorced or have parents who are divorced, and

_____ % live in single-parent homes. Of these single parents, _____ % are women.

The average family in _____'s world has _____ children

(total number of children divided by 10). _____ % of the mothers have jobs outside

the home. _____ % of women with children under the age of six have part-time or

full-time jobs. And _____ % of women with school-aged children work outside
the home. If it became necessary for these women to support their families on their

income alone, _____ % could probably do it in their present jobs.

With a sample as small as the one you just used, the results of your survey may not accurately represent the state of our society in general. As you take the following quizzes, compare your statistics to ours. Is your world a fair reflection of the way Americans live today? If not, pay close attention to the real figures. Remind yourself from time to time that things are not always as they seem.

REALITY #1
Working Women

Our society and our economy have changed drastically in the past few years, and there is no turning back. How aware are you of present conditions regarding women in the workforce? The more you know, the better your chances are of being prepared. Choose what you think are the correct answers to the questions below.

1. The percentage of married working women with children under six years of age increased by what percentage between 1972 and 1982?
    a. 52%
    b. 17%
    c. 36%
    d. 24%

2. The percentage of divorced, widowed or separated working women with children under 18 years of age increased _____ percent between 1972 and 1982.
    a. 56%
    b. 24%
    c. 74%
    d. 36%

3. In 1984, what percentage of women with children under the age of one year were working for pay outside the home?
    a. 7%
    b. 14%
    c. 25%
    d. 46.8%

4. According to the Department of Labor, the average woman works _____ years outside the home.
    a. 26
    b. 12
    c. 4
    d. 19

5. In March, 1984, _____ million men and _____ million women in the U.S. were the only wage earners in their families.
    a. 6 million men and 6 million women
    b. 24 million men and 6 million women
    c. 16 million men and 6 million women
    d. 11 million men and 6 million women

6. Among all American families in March, 1984, _____ was maintained by a woman.
    a. one out of 6
    b. one out of 10
    c. one out of 12
    d. one out of 15

7. About _____ of all families maintained by a woman have incomes below the poverty line.
    a. one-half
    b. one-third
    c. one-eighth
    d. one-quarter

8. Women maintain _____ percent of all black families in America.
    a. 44%
    b. 10%
    c. 36%
    d. 28%

9. _____ percent of all single parents are women.
    a. 75%
    b. 20%
    c. 90%
    d. 50%

10. Thirty years ago, more than 60% of U.S. families consisted of a man working outside the home and a woman at home taking care of children. Today that description fits _____ percent of the households.
    a. 9.9%
    b. 48.8%
    c. 28.3%
    d. 37.2%

Answers follow.

29

How Did You Do?

Correct answers for the quiz are as follows.

1. The number of married working women with children under six years of age increased by: **(a) 52% between 1972 and 1982.**[1] Most of these women went to work because they needed the money. Economic conditions during these years worsened so that it was no longer possible for most families to live on one income. Those conditions show no sign of changing.

2. The number of divorced, widowed or separated working women with children under 18 years of age increased: **(c) 74% between 1971 and 1982.**[2] Though economic conditions would have forced many of these women into the workforce anyway, a soaring divorce rate also began to affect society. As no-fault divorce laws took effect, separated and divorced women could not depend on their ex-husbands for support. These newly single parents were often unprepared to hold jobs that paid more than minimum wage. The feminization of poverty was beginning.

3. In 1984: **(d) 46.8% of women with children under the age of one year were working outside the home.**[3] Many of these women did not return to work out of choice. Their families needed their income. In addition, there is no mandatory maternity leave in this country. Policies vary from place to place. In some instances, a woman can take off only as much time as her accumulated sick leave allows. The most generous companies usually provide for no more than six months away from the office. Some companies guarantee that you will have the same job when you return to work, but most make no such promise.

4. According to the Department of Labor, the average American woman now works: **(a) 26 years outside the home.**[4] There are a number of reasons for this. Women are marrying at a later age. Because of the high cost of living, families are getting smaller. Divorce is more prevalent. More women are not marrying at all.

5. In March, 1984: **(d) 11 million men and 6 million women were the only wage earners in their families.**[5] This figure illustrates the dramatic changes which have taken place in society. While men are generally raised to believe that they will be the family provider, women often are not. The truth is, though, that for every two men who support a family alone, there is now a woman in the same position.

6. Among all American families in March, 1984: **(a) one out of 6 was maintained by a woman.**[6] A woman's chances of being the sole support of her family at some point in her life are very good.

7. About: **(b) one third of all families maintained by a woman have incomes below the poverty line.**[7] Many of these women never expected to find themselves in this situation. They grew up believing in many of the myths we talked about earlier. As a result, they were unprepared to take financial responsibility for themselves, much less for their families.

8. Women maintain: **(a) 44% of all black families in America.**[8] A black woman's chance of being the family provider is almost equal to that of a black man.

9. **(c) 90% of all single parents are women.**[9] And, no matter what anyone says, two (or three or four) **cannot** live as cheaply as one. Most single mothers receive little or no financial support from the fathers of their children. They are on their own, for better or worse.

10. Today, only: **(a) 9.9% of U.S. households consist of a man working outside the home and a woman at home taking care of children.**[10] Can you afford to believe that you will be part of this ever-decreasing population group?

REALITY #2
The Child Care Crunch

The answers to the following questions may startle you. (Remember, answers represent national averages.)

1. About _____ % of American women become mothers at some point in their lives.
   a. 60%
   b. 70%
   c. 80%
   d. 90%

2. According to federal law, pregnant women must be allowed a maternity leave of up to _____.
   a. one month.
   b. six months.
   c. one year.
   d. No maternity leave is required.

3. About _____ % of corporations offer on-site child care.
   a. 1%
   b. 10%
   c. 25%
   d. 50%

4. There are about _____ children under the age of six with working parents in the U.S.
   a. 8.5 million
   b. 3.3 million
   c. 6.8 million
   d. 5.2 million

5. Of those women who work outside the home, _____ % hold **full-time** jobs.
   a. 33%
   b. 71%
   c. 66%
   d. 50%

6. Child care in a private day care **center**, when available, costs about _____ per child per week.
   a. $20 to $50
   b. $80 to $200
   c. $50 to $150
   d. $35 to $75

7. The average single mother earns $_____ per year.
   a. $20,000
   b. $18,000
   c. $9,000
   d. $12,000

8. Child care in a family day care **home** costs about _____ per child per week.
   a. $40 to $70
   b. $25 to $50
   c. $50 to $100
   d. $30 to $60

9. A full-time babysitter at home costs about _____ per week.
   a. $120 to $250
   b. $75 to $100
   c. $100 to $150
   d. $60 to $120

10. About _____ children between the ages of 6 and 13 have no adult supervision for several hours each day because both parents are working.
    a. half a million
    b. one million
    c. one million to two million
    d. two million to five million

Answers follow.

Score Yourself

1. About: (d) 90% of American women become mothers at some point in their lives.[11] Since most women also work outside the home, child care is needed for millions of children every day.

2. (d) There is no mandatory maternity leave in this country. The United States is one of the few western nations that does not provide legal protection for the financial and physical well-being of pregnant women and families with young children. Some employers offer maternity leaves of up to six months, but in most cases women must make their own arrangement for returning to work.

3. Only about: (a) 1% of corporations offer on-site child care.[12] These are usually high-tech industries that employ well-trained workers whose skills are in demand. In other words, if your company needs your particular skill, it will be more willing to accommodate your needs (if it is large enough to do so).

4. There are about: (a) 8.5 million children under the age of six with working parents in the U.S. Day care centers care for only about 10% of them.[13]

5. (b) 71% of working women hold full-time jobs.[14] So, although children are in school, they are in need of some kind of outside care for several hours a day.

6. Private day care **centers** charge about: (b) $80 to $200 per child per week. The cost is too high for many middle-class families, much less those that are truly financially strapped.

7. The average single mother earns about: (c) $9,000 per year.[15] Clearly, she is unable to pay for a day care center. Some subsidized care is available, but not nearly enough to meet the needs of all poor women and children.

8. Child care in a family day care **home** costs about: (a) $40 to $70 per child per week. This is still high for the woman who is earning a minimum wage, but a two-income family can generally afford it. About 40% of working families use this kind of care.[16] Only about 10% of the day care homes are licensed, however, and the quality of care is uneven.

9. Having a full-time babysitter in your home costs from: (a) $120 to $250 a week. Only about 5% of working women can afford this kind of care.[17]

10. (d) There are between two and five million "latchkey" children in America.[18] These six- to thirteen-year-olds are on their own between the time school lets out and the time their parents come home from work.

Perhaps because many people still believe in the myths about sex roles and family, child care is a major problem for any woman hoping or needing to mix career and family. There simply are not enough facilities to care for all of the children who need it. What help there is is generally expensive. Often, it is unreliable. And most businesses still seem to believe that employees and parents are two separate sets of people. They make few concessions to the needs of parents and children.

Talk to a Single Mother

A single mother is a good source of information, not just on the child care crunch, but on a wide range of economic, social and psychological issues. Talk to one. You shouldn't have much trouble locating her. While, in 1970, 11 percent of American children could expect to spend part of their childhood in a single-parent household, 40 to 50 percent of children born in the past ten years will at some point live with just one parent.[19] In 90 percent of these cases, that parent is the mother. What is it like to be a single mother? Ask your subject the following questions.

NAME _____ AGE (OPTIONAL) _____

NUMBER OF CHILDREN _____ AGES _____

EMPLOYED? _____ IF YES, JOB TITLE _____

HOURS WORKED PER WEEK _____ MONTHLY SALARY (OPTIONAL) _____

How long have you been single? _____

When you were growing up, did you ever think you would be raising your children by yourself?
_____

How satisfied are you with your current lifestyle? _____

What are your greatest frustrations? _____

How could your life be easier? _____
_____

If you had your first 25 years to live over, what would you do differently? _____
_____

What advice are you going to give your daughter or another special young woman in your life?
_____
_____

What advice would you give me now? _____
_____

Talk to a Single Father

Being a single parent is difficult for both fathers and mothers, although not always for the same reasons. Interview a single father to see how he feels and what his life is like. Compare the answers from your interviews. How are they alike? How are they different?

NAME _____ AGE (OPTIONAL) _____

NUMBER OF CHILDREN _____ AGES _____

EMPLOYED? _____ IF YES, JOB TITLE _____

HOURS WORKED PER WEEK _____ MONTHLY SALARY (OPTIONAL) _____

How long have you been single? _____

When you were growing up, did you ever think you would be raising your children by yourself?
_____

How satisfied are you with your current lifestyle? _____

What are your greatest frustrations? _____

How could your life be easier? _____
_____

If you had your first 25 years to live over, what would you do differently? _____
_____

What advice are you going to give your child or another special young person in your life?
_____
_____

What advice would you give me now? _____
_____

REALITY #3

"Poverty is Only a Divorce Away"

The "feminization of poverty" is an unsettling term that we are hearing more and more these days. It refers to a dramatic shift in the economic make-up of our country. In the past, there were about an equal number of men and women living in poverty. Now, the majority of poor people in our country are women and children. There are several social and economic reasons for this distressing trend. As you learned earlier in the chapter, most families now need two incomes to maintain a middle-class lifestyle. But an increasing number of families are breaking up. And an increasing number of women have children when they are not married. In 1980, there was one divorce for every two marriages.[20] When there are children in the family, they usually end up living with their mother. And most women do not earn enough to support them.

Can you answer the following questions about the feminization of poverty?

1. _____% of divorced women are single parents.
    a. 10%
    b. 25%
    c. 50%
    d. 60%

2. Within a year after divorce, a man can expect his standard of living
    a. to go up about 42%.
    b. to go down about 10%.
    c. to go up about 20%.
    d. to stay about the same.

3. Within a year after divorce, a woman can expect her standard of living
    a. to stay about the same.
    b. to go down about 73%.
    c. to go up about 10%.
    d. to go down about 25%.

4. After divorce, about _____% of children in the custody of their mothers never see their fathers.
    a. 2%
    b. 11%
    c. 23%
    d. 49%

5. After divorce, about _____ of fathers continue to support their children.
    a. three-fourths
    b. one-third
    c. two-thirds
    d. one-half

6. After divorce, about _____% of women receive alimony.
    a. 80 to 90%
    b. 50 to 75%
    c. 5 to 10%
    d. 20 to 40%

7. About _____ of the poor people in the U.S. today are women and their children.
    a. 77%
    b. 98%
    c. 65%
    d. 58%

8. Working women in America earn about _____% of what men earn.
    a. 100%
    b. 75%
    c. 64%
    d. 50%

Answers follow.

How Did You Do?

1. (d) About 60% of divorced women are single parents.[21] The biggest problem for many divorced women is how to support their children financially. Too often, the problem is unresolved, and both mother and children live in poverty indefinitely.

2. After divorce, a man can expect his standard of living: (a) to go **up** about 42%.[22] Even if he pays child support, the amount is usually less than it **actually** costs to provide for his children. And, in most cases, he has no responsibility at all to help support his ex-wife.

3. After divorce, a woman can expect her standard of living: (b) to go **down** about 73%.[23] Since she almost always has the children, she needs to provide child care. She probably needs a bigger house or apartment than her ex-husband, and she has to feed and clothe the children, pay their medical costs, provide entertainment for them, and so on. And she probably has to do all this on a salary much smaller than that of her ex-husband.

4. After divorce, about: (d) 49% of children in the custody of their mothers never see their fathers.[24] Sometimes ex-wives do not allow visitation. Sometimes one parent relocates and the children are not easily accessible. But in a disturbing number of cases, fathers simply walk out of the lives of their children forever.

5. After divorce, about: (b) one-third of fathers continue to support their children.[25] Therefore, about two-thirds of divorced mothers are solely responsible for the financial support of the family.

6. After divorce, about: (c) 5 to 10% of women receive alimony.[26] As a result of no-fault divorce laws in most states, men are almost never forced to support their ex-wives. Even when alimony is granted, it is usually paid for a limited time, supposedly to allow the woman time to find a job, or be trained for one.

7. About: (a) 77% of the poor people in America today are women and children.[27] Economic conditions, divorce, and single parenting all leave women in an extremely precarious financial position.

8. Women earn about: (c) 64% of what men earn. Even though women are entering many professions previously dominated by men, and even though the subject has received a great deal of attention, this figure has remained constant. In 1983, the average salary for all men was $22,410; for all women, $14,192; for white men, $23,010; for black men, $16,387; for white women, $14,359, and for black women, $12,829.[28]

Go back and count the times the term "after divorce" appeared in this quiz. There is a direct relationship between divorce and the feminization of poverty. While no woman believes that *her* marriage will end in divorce, it is a fact that many do. Remember, too, that a woman can become the sole support of her family if her husband dies, is sick or injured, or loses his job. For all these reasons, it is essential that women today be as well prepared to provide for their families as they expect their husbands to be. Young women who choose motherhood without marriage have an extra responsibility to be able to earn a living.

Review your scores for all three quizzes and then look back at your informal survey on page 28.

How do the figures in your poll compare to national statistics? _____

_____

How much of the material in the quizzes was new to you? _____

_____

What did you find most surprising? _____

_____

REALITY #4

Equal, But Different

For years, women in the United States have struggled to be treated fairly and as men's equals. A quick look at some of the facts we've just discussed reveals that the struggle has not been entirely successful. In some cases, social and economic changes have actually worsened conditions for women and children. Government, business, and the family structure itself have been slow to catch up with the different roles women now play. For example:

> **Government** has been slow to enforce laws requiring equal pay for equal work and affirmative action (hiring and promoting women and minorities in percentages equal to their percentage of the population). Efforts to pass comparable worth laws (equal pay for work requiring equal training or equal responsibility) have not been supported by those in power. Employers are not required to provide maternity leave in America, and there is not enough affordable or subsidized day care. In addition, present divorce laws are not stringent enough to make men take some financial responsibility for their children.
>
> **Business,** in general, does not accommodate the needs of parents of either sex. Only about 40% of working women are covered by some kind of maternity leave.[29] Inflexible hours make it difficult to care for children. And women are still paid less than men in almost every field.
>
> **The family** doesn't exactly rush to Mom's support, either. Studies show that women are still largely responsible for both child care and housework, even when they have full-time jobs outside the home.

A Society in Transition

Some of these problems are slowly being remedied and, as time goes by and women's efforts continue, more advances will be made. In times of great social and economic change, institutions have a hard time keeping pace. In the final chapter of this book, we will discuss some things you might want to do to help the transition take place.

In the meantime, though, you will be responsible for your own situation. This chapter has dealt mainly with the crises women face today. But there are opportunities, as well. Unlike women of the past generations, you are free to combine career and family life. You will not be barred from the career of your choice simply because of your sex. If you want to be a politician or an astronaut, an athlete or an artist, an engineer, police officer, or plumber, you can find role models to guide or inspire you. If you know what you want from your life, and if you are willing to work for it, this can be an exciting and rewarding time.

Men, too, have much to gain from these changes. With financial help from a working partner, men have more freedom to change jobs or careers, or to work at something they find meaningful, even if it doesn't pay top dollar. Many men are taking a more active role in parenting. They have interests outside of their jobs. And all this seems to make them healthier and happier people.

Before you go on to the next chapter, however, take a few minutes to reflect on the things you've just learned.

What do you find most disturbing about the realities of women's lives today? _____
_____

What opportunities do you see for improvement? _____
_____

Do the statistics in this chapter accurately reflect the lives of women you know? _____
_____

What do you think government should do to make life easier for parents and children? _____
_____

What do you think business should do to help the parents of young children? _____
_____

What do you think men should do to help their wives? _____
_____

What do you think divorced men should do to help their children and ex-wives? _____
_____

What do you think women should do to help themselves? _____
_____

Maybe you don't have all the answers to these questions now. We hope, though, that by the time you finish this book, you will have a better understanding of the issues, how they affect you personally, and what kinds of solutions might be beneficial for society as a whole.

The Need for Careful Planning

This book is subtitled "A Strategic Planning Guide for Mixing Career and Family." Think about that for a minute. The dictionary defines "strategic" as something "essential to the effective conduct of war." That may sound a little strong to you, but the fact is that women today are fighting difficult battles against discrimination, poverty and exhaustion. We do not want you to be a victim in this struggle. If you want to come out a winner, there are three initial steps you need to make.

> **First,** you need to consider the facts. What is the world like? There are some things you can do to change it, but there are other forces you simply cannot control. As you make decisions about your future, it is important to take these realities into consideration.
>
> **Secondly,** think carefully about the kind of life you want. What kind of work will you find rewarding? Do you want to marry? To have children? What do you believe in? What things in life are most important to you? What skills and attitudes do you need to meet your goals? Do you have them? Can you get them?
>
> **Finally, start planning now to give yourself the best chance of success. Careful planning is the key.**
>
> In the next few years, you will make decisions that will affect the rest of your life. They should be made thoughtfully and deliberately, with conscious awareness of the kind of life you will find most satisfying. The rest of this book will help you develop your plan.

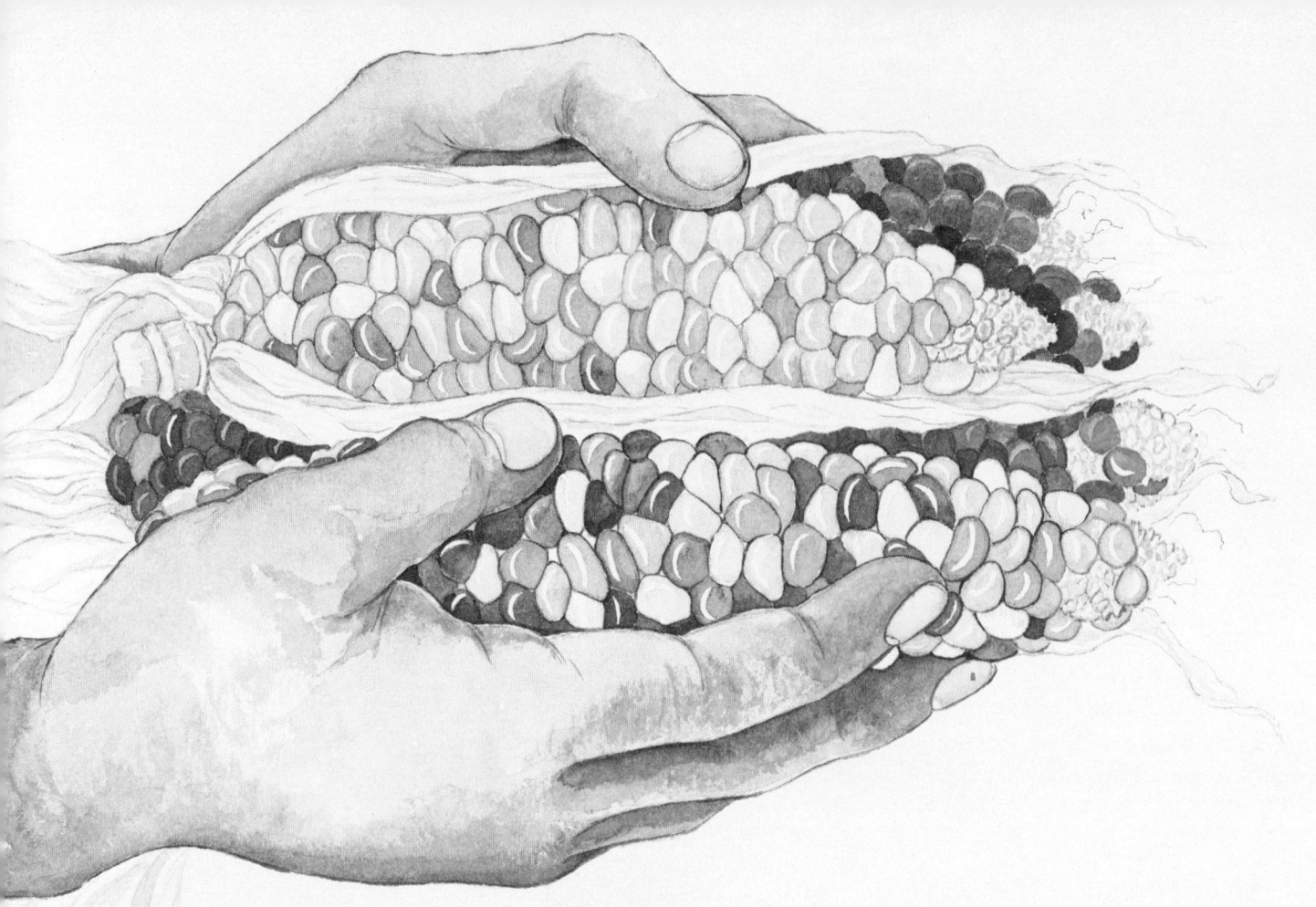

REFLECTIONS

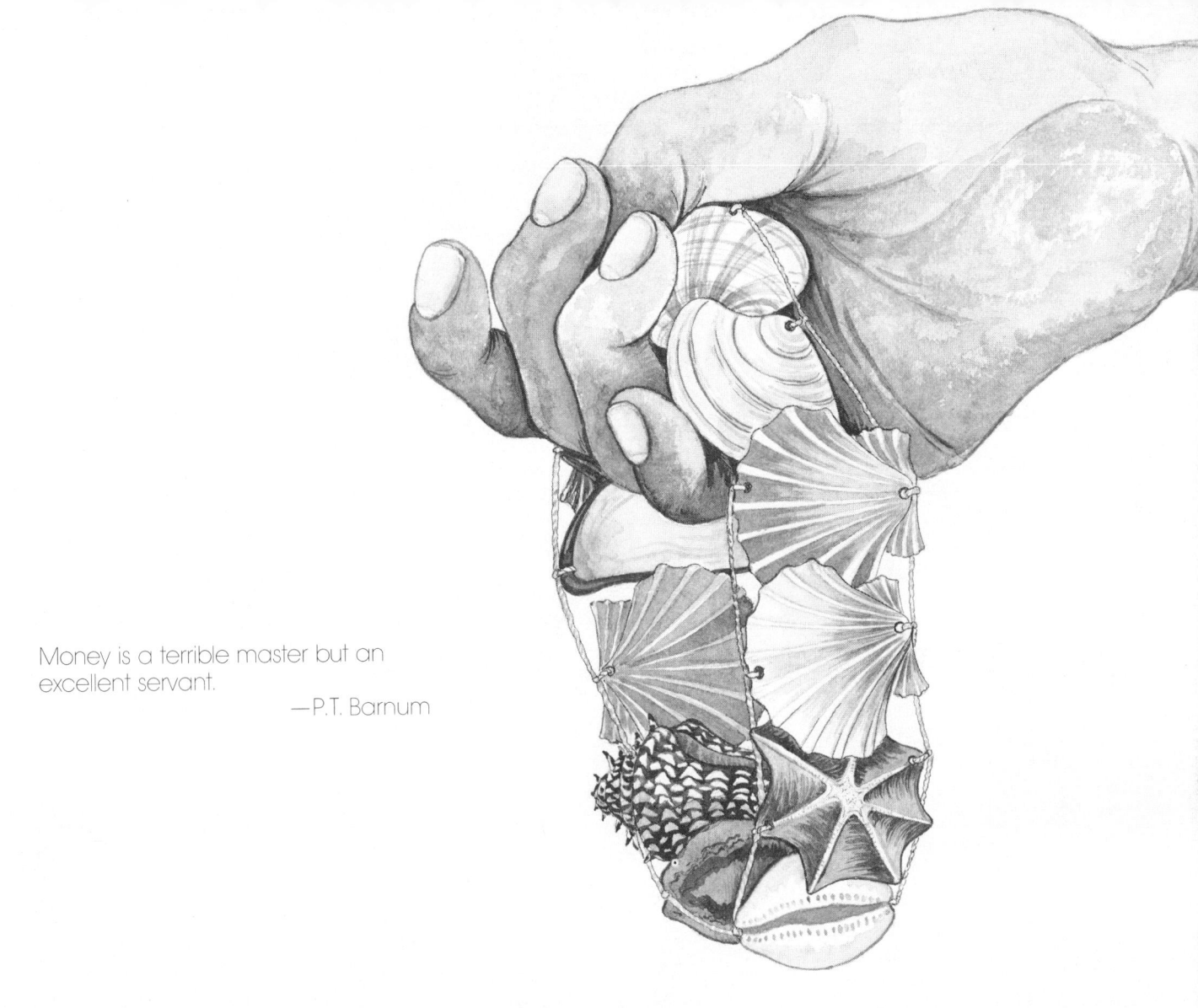

Money is a terrible master but an excellent servant.
—P.T. Barnum

Chapter Three

Money: How Important Is It?

Very few people can afford to be poor.
—George Bernard Shaw

Melody's Story

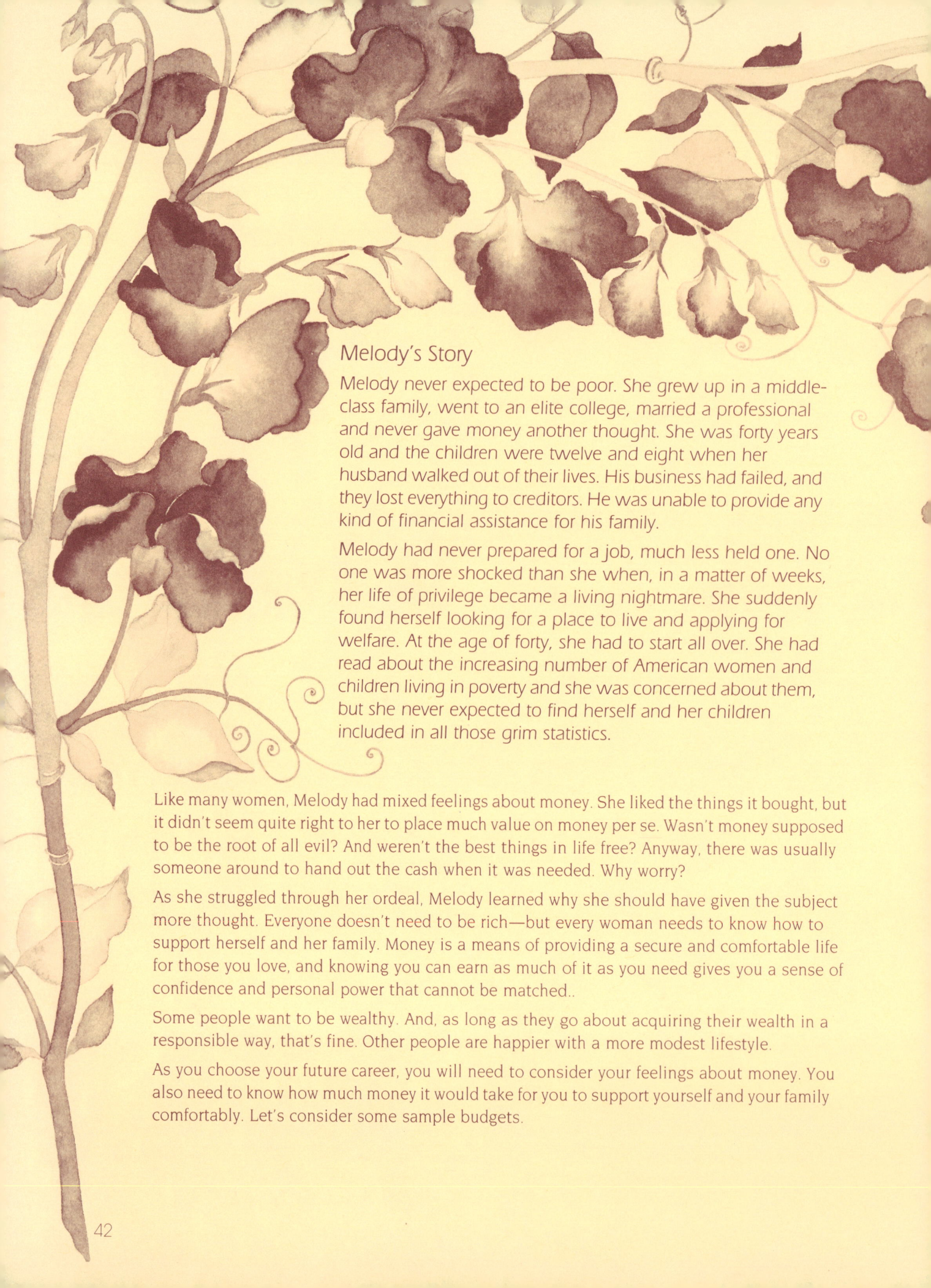

Melody never expected to be poor. She grew up in a middle-class family, went to an elite college, married a professional and never gave money another thought. She was forty years old and the children were twelve and eight when her husband walked out of their lives. His business had failed, and they lost everything to creditors. He was unable to provide any kind of financial assistance for his family.

Melody had never prepared for a job, much less held one. No one was more shocked than she when, in a matter of weeks, her life of privilege became a living nightmare. She suddenly found herself looking for a place to live and applying for welfare. At the age of forty, she had to start all over. She had read about the increasing number of American women and children living in poverty and she was concerned about them, but she never expected to find herself and her children included in all those grim statistics.

Like many women, Melody had mixed feelings about money. She liked the things it bought, but it didn't seem quite right to her to place much value on money per se. Wasn't money supposed to be the root of all evil? And weren't the best things in life free? Anyway, there was usually someone around to hand out the cash when it was needed. Why worry?

As she struggled through her ordeal, Melody learned why she should have given the subject more thought. Everyone doesn't need to be rich—but every woman needs to know how to support herself and her family. Money is a means of providing a secure and comfortable life for those you love, and knowing you can earn as much of it as you need gives you a sense of confidence and personal power that cannot be matched..

Some people want to be wealthy. And, as long as they go about acquiring their wealth in a responsible way, that's fine. Other people are happier with a more modest lifestyle.

As you choose your future career, you will need to consider your feelings about money. You also need to know how much money it would take for you to support yourself and your family comfortably. Let's consider some sample budgets.

Melody's Budget

If Melody and her children lived in California, she could expect to receive a total of about $700 a month in AFDC (Aid to Families with Dependent Children, often referred to as "welfare") and Food Stamps. Here's how Melody might budget that amount.

ITEM	AMOUNT	DESCRIPTION
Rent or mortgage	$350	One-bedroom apartment, run-down neighborhood, poor condition
Utilities	$ 50	Little heat, no air conditioning or phone, no cable TV
Insurance	$ 0	None
Transportation	$ 25	Bus fare
Food	$160*	Lots of spaghetti and bread, little meat or fresh fruits and vegetables
Child care	$ 15	One night out a month for Melody, sometimes help from family or friends
Clothing	$ 60	Mostly necessities from the secondhand store
Entertainment	$ 40	Melody's night out, plus McDonald's or a pizza with the kids each month
		Saving for a used TV
Medical	$ 0	Government subsidy
Vacations	$ 0	None
Gifts and contributions	$ 0	None
TOTAL	$700	

Would you be happy with this lifestyle? _____

*or what food stamps allow

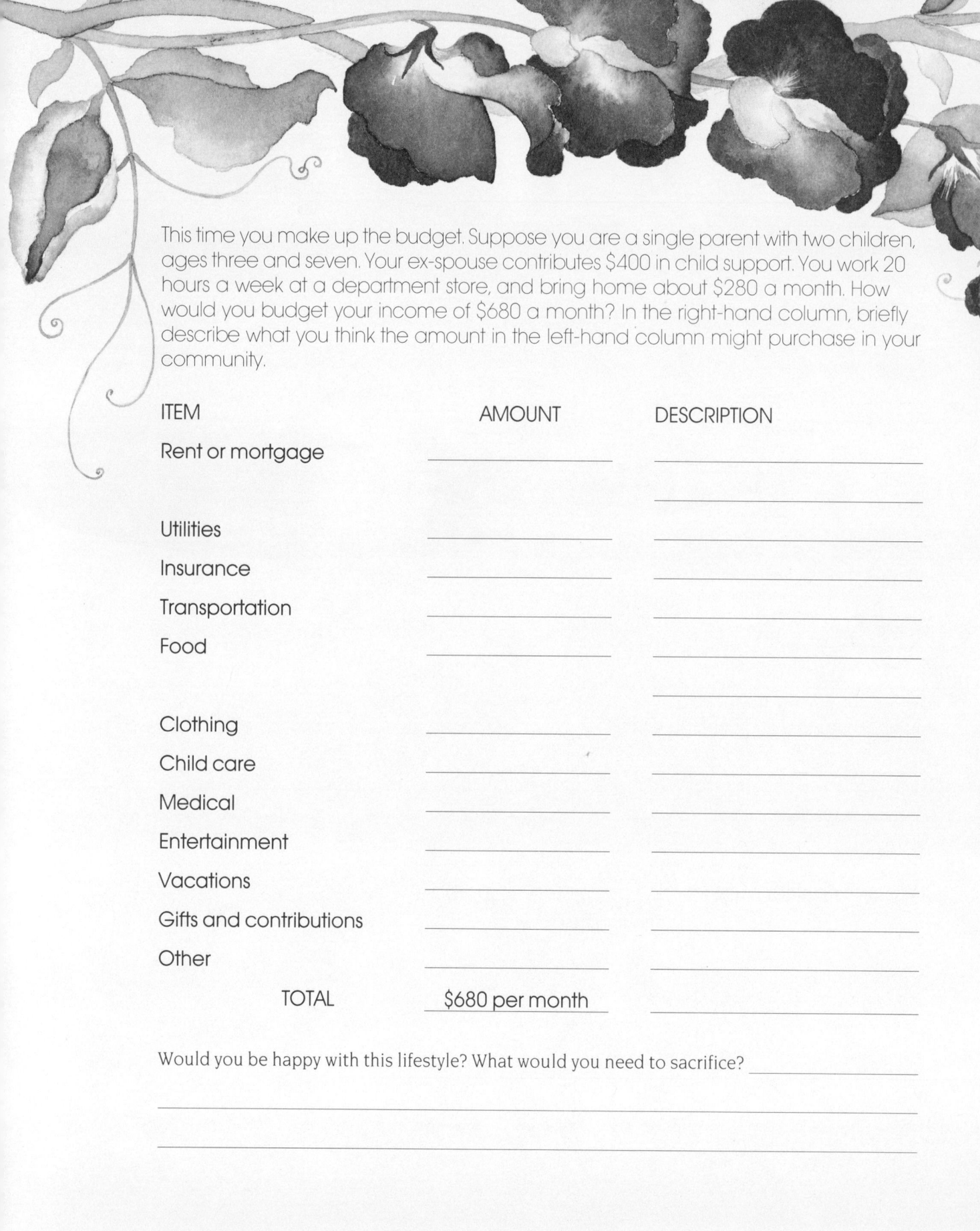

This time you make up the budget. Suppose you are a single parent with two children, ages three and seven. Your ex-spouse contributes $400 in child support. You work 20 hours a week at a department store, and bring home about $280 a month. How would you budget your income of $680 a month? In the right-hand column, briefly describe what you think the amount in the left-hand column might purchase in your community.

ITEM	AMOUNT	DESCRIPTION
Rent or mortgage	_____	_____
		_____
Utilities	_____	_____
Insurance	_____	_____
Transportation	_____	_____
Food	_____	_____
		_____
Clothing	_____	_____
Child care	_____	_____
Medical	_____	_____
Entertainment	_____	_____
Vacations	_____	_____
Gifts and contributions	_____	_____
Other	_____	_____
TOTAL	$680 per month	_____

Would you be happy with this lifestyle? What would you need to sacrifice? _____
_____
_____

Now suppose you are a parent in the same situation, only this time you bring home $1,400 a month from your job as a social studies teacher. Your ex-spouse still pays $400 a month in child support. Determine a budget for a family with a monthly net income of $1,800.

ITEM	AMOUNT	DESCRIPTION
Rent or mortgage		
Utilities		
Insurance		
Transportation		
Food		
Clothing		
Child care		
Medical		
Entertainment		
Vacations		
Gifts and contributions		
Savings		
Other		
TOTAL	$1,800 per month	

Would this lifestyle make you happy? What would you sacrifice? _____

One more time. This time you're an electrical engineer bringing home $2,200 a month. You still have the same children and receive the same $400 in monthly child support. Complete your $2,600 budget.

ITEM	AMOUNT	DESCRIPTION
Rent or mortgage	_____	_____
		_____
Utilities	_____	_____
Insurance	_____	_____
Food	_____	_____
		_____
Clothing	_____	_____
Child care	_____	_____
Transportation	_____	_____
Dental and medical	_____	_____
Entertainment	_____	_____
Vacations	_____	_____
Gifts and contributions	_____	_____
Savings	_____	_____
Other	_____	_____
TOTAL	$2,600 per month	

Would you be happy with this lifestyle?_____

What would you have to sacrifice?_____

Which of these families do you suppose would be most comfortable?_____

Which would probably have the most disagreements?_____

Which parent would probably feel most in control of the situation?_____

Which could feel secure that the children were being well cared for?_____

What Does Money Mean To You?

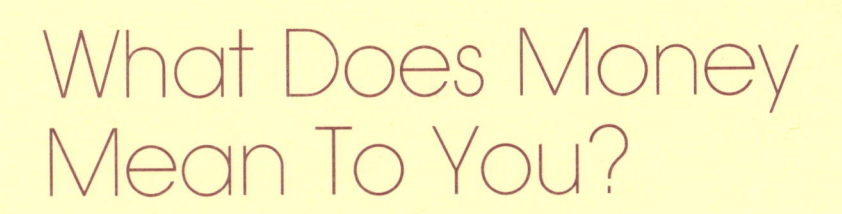

If you attended a class reunion, or any gathering of old friends, you would probably witness an interesting phenomenon. People would be openly sharing stories about their jobs and families, their health, their hobbies, even their religious and political beliefs. The topic of money, however, would be avoided. If you brought it up, your listeners would probably look startled, change the subject, or suddenly spot someone on the other side of the room they needed to speak to immediately.

And yet money has an enormous impact on our lives. It can be used in many ways, both good and bad. If you are to use it well—to get the most satisfaction from it—you need to decide what money means to you as you plan your future life.

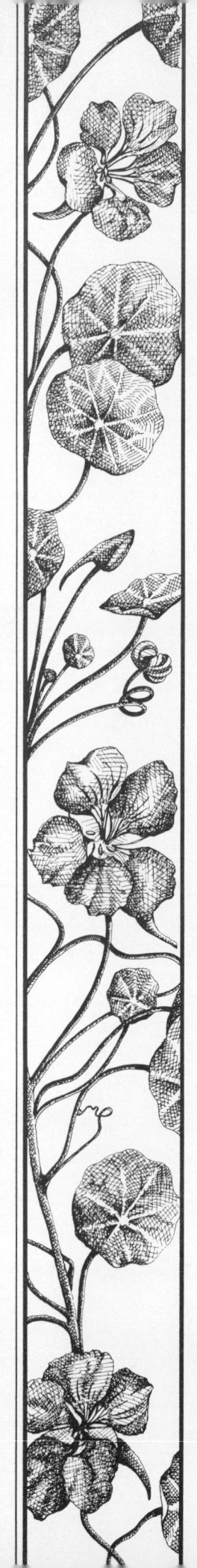

If the people at the class reunion had been willing to talk about money, they might have revealed feelings similar to these:

VALENCIA thinks of money as some kind of magic carpet that will soon allow her to escape from her family of eight younger brothers and sisters, every one of them a monster. Money, she says, means independence.

TOM considers money a security blanket. He was poor once, and he's determined not to be in that position again. Every time he gets paid, he puts a large portion of his check in his savings account.

RHONDA knows the power money can lend her, and she likes it. People return her phone calls, ask her to sit on committees, give her the best tables in restaurants.

BONNIE thinks of money as a status symbol. She likes having her name in the newspapers, her children in the most exclusive schools, and her vacations in the trendiest locations.

JEROME likes to buy things. He says shopping is his hobby, and as long as he can pay for what he buys, no one has a right to criticize him.

COZETTE likes to play games with money, very profitable games as a rule. She knows a lot about investing, and uses her money to make more money.

YOLANDA is a giver. She buys lavish gifts for her friends, but also gets a thrill out of giving money to her favorite charities and cultural organizations.

ANTHONY doesn't care for money at all. He prefers to live simply and earn what he needs by bartering his work for goods and services from others.

YOKO uses money as a measuring stick. She likes to compare how much she earned this year with how much she earned in previous years to gauge how well she is doing in her career.

RAFAELA uses her money to buy time. If she can hire other people to run her errands, clean her house, and cook her meals, she has that much more time to do the things that are important to her.

JEAN gets sick to her stomach whenever she has to think about money. There is never enough to stretch to the end of the month, no matter how carefully she budgets.

NICK exchanges money for leisure. He tries to take one major trip and several shorter vacations every year.

SUE isn't sure what to think about money. She knows she needs it, but doesn't feel entirely comfortable handling it. It just doesn't seem right.

SYLVIA hates money. The need for it has only brought suffering. Her inability to meet her family's needs makes her feel so inadequate.

What about you? What do you think about money? The following exercise should help you clarify your thoughts.

INCOME EXPECTATION SURVEY

To see what you expect money to do for you, check the column that most closely matches your feelings as you consider this list of statements. Remember that your expectations are subject to change from time to time. You may want to take this quiz several times during the next few years, as you continue to plan for your future.

		Very True	Sometimes True	Not Sure	Not True
1.	I believe that a percentage of my income should be spent to help others.				
2.	I feel a person's salary indicates how much she or he is valued on the job.				
3.	I would rather have a large savings account than a large home.				
4.	I wish I had enough money to do whatever I wanted for a year.				
5.	I would rather buy something I have always wanted than join a private club.				
6.	I would rather join a private club than buy something I have always wanted.				
7.	I am just as happy eating hamburger as steak.				
8.	When I see something I want, I want to be able to buy it immediately.				
9.	If I had enough money, I would retire now and enjoy life.				
10.	I'd like to be able to put my children through college on my own.				
11.	I like to be recognized as a person with power.				
12.	I am just as happy buying my clothes at Sears as in the designer section at the department store.				
13.	I'd like to set up a foundation and give money to causes I support.				
14.	I could tell you my total net worth anytime you ask.				
15.	I worry about my old age and having enough money to retire on.				
16.	I would rather drive a new car than have money in a savings account.				
17.	I like to collect all the newest gadgets.				
18.	I wish I could send my parents on their dream vacation.				
19.	As long as my home is safe and comfortable, I don't care how big or fancy it is.				
20.	I feel it's important to help those less fortunate than I am.				
21.	If I lost money in the stock market, the fact that I failed would bother me more than the money lost.				

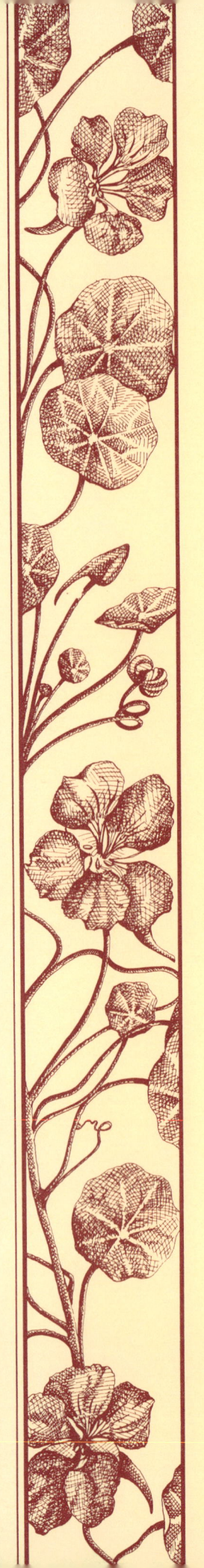

	Very True	Sometimes True	Not Sure	Not True
22. I enjoy the excitement of investing my money and watching it grow.				
23. I'd rather have time than money.				
24. I will contribute to my own retirement account before I buy household extras.				
25. I want to buy a new car every year.				
26. I want to associate with influential people.				
27. I would donate to charity because of the recognition it would bring.				
28. I like to be surrounded by beautiful things.				
29. I think it's important to make monthly deposits in my savings account.				
30. I would not work for a company that didn't offer medical insurance.				
31. I would stay home and be a full-time parent even if it meant never owning a house.				
32. When I save enough money, I would rather start my own business than buy a luxury item.				
33. I'd rather have my savings in a bank account than in a stock account.				
34. I can tell how well I'm doing at my job by how much money I make.				
35. It's important that my job helps others, even if I have to take a lower salary.				
36. I think material things just tie you down and give you more work to do.				
37. I wouldn't want to make money at something if it meant that others would lose theirs.				
38. I would donate to a political campaign in order to have a connection with the candidate				
39. I want my child to attend a prestigious university.				
40. I would rather shop than save money.				
41. It's more important to me to be debt-free than to buy new clothes on my credit cards.				
42. It would be great to have 100 people working for me.				
43. I don't want the responsibility of being boss.				
44. I believe that you can't take it (money) with you.				
45. The most important thing about owning your own business is the freedom it allows.				
46. I feel smart and successful when my investments do well.				
47. I don't like to think about money.				
48. I believe that money can't buy love or happiness.				
49. When I lend money to a friend, I don't worry about getting paid back.				

	Very True	Some-times True	Not Sure	Not True
50. I wish someone else would take responsibility for my financial situation.				
51. I like to be waited on — it makes me feel important.				
52. I don't want to have to worry about losing my job.				
53. I'd rather have household help to give me more free time than buy a luxury item I've always wanted.				
54. I'd rather have a pay raise than a more prestigious title.				
55. I'd rather donate monthly to a community homeless project than make a monthly payment on a new stereo.				
56. As long as my car runs and is safe, I don't care what it looks like.				
57. I like to be recognized in a large group.				
58. I believe when the going gets tough, the tough go shopping.				
59. I believe that a penny saved is a penny earned.				
60. I'd rather make sacrifices to save money when I'm young so I can afford to retire early or start my own business.				
61. I like being able to decide for myself how I will spend my time.				
62. When I take on increased job responsibilities I expect a pay raise.				
63. The feeling I get when I donate to a good cause is better than the feeling I get from an evening on the town.				
64. I can enjoy a beautiful sunset as much as an expensive concert.				
65. It is very important to me that my salary be higher than those of my former classmates.				
66. I believe the best things in life are free				
67. In order to be happy at my job, I must believe I'm being paid what I'm worth.				
68. I'd rather be the boss than the worker.				
69. I don't want to worry about whether or not I can afford it when I purchase something.				
70. I would like to travel first class because of the attention I would get and the influential people I would meet.				
71. In my fantasies, I covet the lifestyles of "Dallas" and "Dynasty."				
72. Just to be able to buy what I *need* when I want it would make me happy.				
73. Sometimes I worry about being unable to support my basic needs.				

	Very True	Sometimes True	Not Sure	Not True
74. I'd like to have enough money to move to a better neighborhood.				
75. I'd like to be the first person in my family to own a house.				
76. It would be great if I could buy my parents a nice house in a decent neighborhood.				
77. As long as there's food on the table, I don't worry about money.				

Which statements are "very true" for you at this time? Find those statement numbers below and write a 9 beside each one. Write a 6 beside the numbers to which you replied "sometimes true," a 3 beside your "not sure" answers, and a 0 by the statements you indicated are "not true." When you have entered a number on each line, total the numbers you have assigned in each category. The category in which you have the highest score reflects your strongest feeling about money right now. Read on to find an explanation of each category.

Helping Others	Measure of Success	Security	Freedom
1 _____	2 _____	3 _____	4 _____
10 _____	14 _____	15 _____	9 _____
13 _____	21 _____	24 _____	23 _____
18 _____	22 _____	29 _____	31 _____
20 _____	34 _____	30 _____	32 _____
35 _____	46 _____	33 _____	45 _____
37 _____	54 _____	41 _____	53 _____
49 _____	62 _____	43 _____	60 _____
55 _____	65 _____	52 _____	61 _____
63 _____	67 _____	59 _____	68 _____
76 _____	75 _____	73 _____	74 _____
Total _____	Total _____	Total _____	Total _____

Purchasing Power	Power and Prestige	Unfortunate Necessity
5 _____	6 _____	7 _____
8 _____	11 _____	12 _____
16 _____	26 _____	19 _____
25 _____	27 _____	36 _____
17 _____	38 _____	47 _____
28 _____	39 _____	48 _____
40 _____	42 _____	50 _____
44 _____	51 _____	56 _____
58 _____	57 _____	64 _____
69 _____	70 _____	66 _____
72 _____	71 _____	77 _____
Total _____	Total _____	Total _____

Helping Others

Some people believe that a desire to have money is selfish, but if you scored high in this category, you know that money can be used to help your family and friends, to support causes you believe in, and to make the world a better place for everyone. How much money you will need depends on the scale of your ambitions. Do you want to be able to be generous with your family and close friends? Do you want to make sizable contributions to charity? Or do you want to set up your own foundation to give money to causes you deem worthy? In any case, you will not want to work in a profession or industry you believe is harmful or unethical. Perhaps you should consider a career in one of the helping professions. Doctors, lawyers, pharmacists and veterinarians are all in the business of doing good for others. You might want to be a counselor or a research scientist, a politician or a diplomat, a farmer, or an engineer. Or you may want to trade a high salary for the intrinsic rewards of knowing you are helping others. There are some satisfactions that no amount of money can buy.

Security

Those who think the best thing about money is the security it provides are probably not cut out to start their own businesses, or to invest their time or money in any kind of risky venture. If you scored highest in this category, you want most of all to make sure that your economic needs will be met, that you don't have to worry about losing your job, your health, or your savings. You will probably want a position with an established firm, or one providing a basic service that is not likely to become obsolete. Government service jobs are generally considered secure. A job with good benefits and a generous pension will suit you best. Your salary need not be *high*, but it must be *adequate*. Only you can judge what is adequate.

Measure of Success

If you scored highest in this category, your motto might be the old saying, "If you're so smart, why aren't you rich?" You think of your salary as a report card: the higher it is, the better you are doing. You want to be at the head of your class. And you may be willing to take calculated risks if the potential for earnings is great enough. People in this category have many career choices. Large corporations offer many fellow employees with whom you can compete, or you might choose to work for yourself, which is a good way to know exactly how you're doing. Many of the professions, too, have official or unofficial ways of indicating how well you are doing in relation to your peers. You might also be interested in investment opportunities, whether as a profession or a hobby. Warning: Women who score high in this category may be frustrated to find that, in many positions, they may be doing better work than their male colleagues but earning less money. Solution: Work for yourself, work with other women, or work to change the system (See chapter 12).

Freedom

People who like the freedom money gives them don't like to be controlled by others. They often find happiness as entrepreneurs, freelancers, consultants, or professionals in private practice. (See Chapter 5 for more information about these career opportunities.) The important thing to them is maintaining their ability to be in charge of their own lives, to do what they want to do. If you scored highest in this category, you are probably not concerned about displaying your wealth for the benefit of others. You will be more likely to spend extra income on travel or for help around the house so you can have more time to do the things you like. Or you may choose a career with a lower salary simply because it offers you more freedom in all areas of your life.

Purchasing Power

If you scored highest in this category, you will want to earn enough money to buy what you want, when you want it. It's important for you to always have the most, the latest, and the best—of everything. A career with a substantial salary is important. Becoming a professional or working in corporate management might meet your financial needs. Or you might be successful as a salesperson. People with an interest in our patterns of consumption might also do well in marketing or advertising. If you can spot trends before everyone else does, you might have the makings of an entrepreneur or a buyer for a major department store. Caution: If this is your highest value, and you do not make a salary that meets your needs, you are in danger of getting caught in the credit card trap.

Power and Prestige

People who score highest in this category like the recognition that money can bring, and the power it can deliver. Money is a status symbol in our society, and people who have it are likely to be treated well. These people can have the material goods they want. They may also have the influence necessary to get other people to do their bidding. If you value money for its power and prestige, you will need to be well off, or at least have a career that lets you associate with wealthy people or prestigious institutions. You might consider a career in one of the professions or in business administration, or you might want to have your own business. It's risky, but the financial rewards can be sizable.

Unfortunate Necessity

People who score high in this category can live simply and happily with a small but adequate income. If you are one of those people, you are lucky—you can accept a job you love even if its pay scale is too low for most people to find satisfactory. Caution: Sometimes women score high in this category because they don't like to think about money, or they assume someone else will be around to help with the bills. Be sure you've carefully thought about your budgets for your present and future life. It's important that you know you and your family could live comfortably on your income *alone*.

Income Expectation and Career Choice

To see how income expectation affects your career choice, complete this exercise. Try to think of careers that would meet the needs of people scoring high in each of the following categories. Then think of careers that *would not* meet those needs. Enter your answers on the lines below.

	Meet expectations	Do not meet expectations
Helping Others	_____	_____
	_____	_____
Measure of Success	_____	_____
	_____	_____
Security	_____	_____
	_____	_____
Freedom	_____	_____
	_____	_____
Purchasing Power	_____	_____
	_____	_____
Power and Prestige	_____	_____
	_____	_____
Unfortunate Necessity	_____	_____
	_____	_____

In which categories did you have the *easiest* time coming up with appropriate careers? Which categories were most *difficult* for you? Can you think of reasons why this is so?

For the most part, people with very high income expectations simply do not have as many options in career choice as do people with more modest income expectations. If money is of no concern to you, you are free to follow your heart and pursue any job you want (as long as it meets your basic financial needs). If power, prestige and "big bucks" are your ideal, you will probably need to work in one of a limited number of career fields. As in all areas of life, there are trade-offs. Only you can decide which route you will find most satisfying.

Assessing Your Career Values

What you expect your income to do for you will greatly influence your career choice. But, of course, there are many other things to consider before you choose your life's work. What job will make you happy? What career will you find most satisfying?

Answer the questions below to help clarify your values in regard to your work. (For more extensive information, see *Choices* or *Challenges*.)

How would you like your life work to fit in with your family life?

_____
_____

Is it important that your job has an element of adventure, or at least that it is not the same, day after day?

_____

Is it important that your job lets you keep learning and growing, or are you more comfortable simply knowing exactly what is expected of you?

_____

Do you prefer to work with others, or alone?

_____

Would you rather work with your mind or your hands?

_____

Is it important to you that your job is one you can be proud of, one that is socially useful? Or can you satisfy that need with volunteer work on your own time?

_____

How much creativity would you like to have in your job?

_____

How important are your surroundings at work? Which surroundings would you find the most pleasing? (plush office, outdoors, home office, working among machines or computers?)

_____
_____

How much responsibility are you willing to accept? Are you comfortable in a leadership role?

_____

What are your particular skills, interests and aptitudes?

_____

How Does Money Affect Your Decisions?

The way you feel about money will often be a factor in the decisions you make for yourself, your job and your family. If you are aware of your feelings, you are more likely to make the most satisfying choices. The following exercise should give you another way of looking at your own preferences. For each of the statements, choose the response you would be most likely to make.

You are 35 years old. Your favorite great-aunt died and left you $20,000. With that money you would most likely:

    a. Join the local country club.
    b. Purchase a _____ that you have always wanted.
                               fill in
    c. Start a savings account.
    d. Quit the job you don't like.
    e. Start an investment account.
    f. Help your younger sister go to graduate school.
    g. Change your life very little—put it away and use it as needed.

You are 35 years old. For the last five years you have worked on an instrument used in the medical field that has been acclaimed throughout the world. You have just sold the patent for 1 million dollars. With that money you would most likely:

    a. Move to an exclusive community and join clubs and groups that are prestigious.
    b. Purchase a _____ that you have always wanted.
                               fill in
    c. Invest in a high interest-bearing account, retire, pursue recreational interests and live off the income.
    d. Buy five years of freedom to travel and expand your knowledge.
    e. Invest in a new business and hire a housekeeper to care for the family.
    f. Become a full-time community activist, donating your time and some money to your cause.
    g. Not let the money change your lifestyle—go right on inventing.

You are 35 years old, married with two children. You are offered a prestigious job that pays double your present salary but requires long hours and frequent travel. You accept the job. Which of the following would most closely reflect your thinking?

a. The status and recognition you will receive are important to you.
b. The extra money will allow the family to live in luxury.
c. You will be able to put away money for retirement or emergency needs.
d. The new job lets you be the boss—you will have more control.
e. The title and the big salary make you feel as if you've "made it".
f. You'll be able to send your kids to the best schools, take care of your aging parents, and support your favorite causes.
g. You would turn the job down, except that your spouse was recently laid off, one of the kids has required some expensive medical care, and you're broke.

In the same situation as described above, you **turn down** the new position for the following reason:

a. Your power and status in the home are more important to you than prestige on the job.
b. You're happy with your current standard of living.
c. You would worry about your spouse and children when you had to work late or travel.
d. It's more important to you to have time for yourself and your family.
e. Just being offered the position makes you feel successful on the job—now you want to devote more effort to being a successful spouse, parent and human being.
f. You'd rather have the time to work for your favorite charities.
g. You work only to meet financial obligations. More money doesn't hold any attraction for you.

You are 35 years old, happily married, with an exciting and financially rewarding career. After thinking the situation through, you have decided to leave your job for an extended period to start your family. You can afford to take about two years off. What part of your job will you miss the most?

    a. Your own secretary, the executive lunchroom, and the company and respect of your fellow employees.

    b. The company car and the expense account for travel.

    c. The security of a steady income of your own.

    d. The freedom your job affords you to do what you want.

    e. The thrill of your regular promotions.

    f. The feeling you have of being valued and needed for your knowledge and skills.

    g. The work itself.

In the same situation, what will worry you the most?

    a. That you will be thought of as less vital and interesting than you were when you worked.

    b. That you might have to give up your credit cards and cut back on spending.

    c. That you won't be able to make ends meet.

    d. That your spouse will be more controlling when you're not earning any money.

    e. That you might never regain the momentum in your career, that you might be permanently stifled in your ambition.

    f. That you might be less valued as a volunteer for your favorite charity than you were as a donor.

    g. That you will miss your work.

Which letter response did you choose most often? Score yourself as follows: Each "a" response reflects power and prestige; each "b" response reflects purchasing power; "c" equals security; "d" indicates a desire for freedom; "e" answers mean you think of money as a measure of success; "f" that you would like to use it to help others; and "g" that you think of money as an unfortunate necessity.

Do your responses in this exercise relate to the results of the income expectation survey? If so, your financial expectations should be clear to you. If not, you need to do some more thinking on the topic. Perhaps you have a totally different view, or you may feel different about money under different circumstances. Turn back to page 54 and read the definitions for each category in which you had a high score on the previous exercise, or responded to more than once on this quiz. Which definition do you agree with most? Keep thinking, and do the exercises again when you have finished the book. Your values can change, but it is important that your feelings about money are compatible with your career and lifestyle goal.

Money Isn't Everything

As you go through life, you will want to ask yourself why money is important to you whenever you need to make a decision which will have an impact on your income or the way you live. Remember, money is not the only measure of the quality of your life. There is a big difference between having a lust for money and being a provider for your family. It is not necessary to be wealthy to enjoy the riches of family, friends and a full, rewarding life.

Remember too, though, that if you choose to have a family, you have a responsibility to provide for their physical well-being. And that might mean making some temporary sacrifices. If you want very much in life to be a published poet, but so far you have only collected a drawer full of rejection slips, you may want to spend a few years earning a living as a teacher or journalist while you provide for your children. (Often your talents can be enriched and polished while earning a living and providing for your family.) When your children are on their own and your sphere of responsibility has changed, you may find that a dream postponed is not necessarily a dream denied.

> I'd rather have roses on my table than diamonds on my neck.
> —Emma Goldman

> Money is a guarantee that we may have what we want in the future. Though we need nothing at the moment it insures the possibility of satisfying a new desire when it arises.
> —Aristotle

> When I think of all the sorrow and the barrenness that has been wrought in my life by want of a few more pounds per annum than I was able to earn, I stand aghast at money's significance.
> —George Gissing

> It's easy to be independent when you have money. But to be independent when you haven't got a thing—that's the Lord's test.
> —Mahalia Jackson

REFLECTIONS

CHAPTER FOUR

A Parent's Limited Resources: Time, Money & Energy

In bringing up children, spend on them half as much money and twice as much time.

Lost time is never found again.
—Benjamin Franklin

Olympia's Story

Olympia planned her future carefully from the day she took her first advanced math class in high school. She was going to be a certified public accountant. She studied hard all through college and was recruited to work for one of the top eight accounting firms as soon as she graduated. As she had always done, she continued to work hard and she continued to advance. Within a few years she was earning $36,000 per year. By the time she was thirty years old, she began planning for a baby. Her husband, Malcolm, could not make many changes in his career to accomodate the new child. But Olympia was ready. She was able to leave the accounting firm and start her own small practice, where she could put in as many—or as few—hours as she needed to.

Olympia's friend, Barbara, was less fortunate. With her advanced degree in social work, she was making only about $21,000 when she and her husband decided to start a family at about the same time as Olympia. She would have liked to work part-time, but the agency she worked for had no provisions for part-time employees. And, frankly, Barbara needed all the income from her full-time job.

Time—Your Finite Resource

Assuming that you will have to make money even when your children are very small, would you rather be in Olympia's position, or in Barbara's? And just how do their positions differ, anyway? Both are hard-working professionals with about the same amount of training. But Olympia earns more money than Barbara does—at a ratio of almost 2 to 1. That fact alone gives Olympia something precious to a young mother—time. She can work fewer hours and still make a comfortable salary.

Because she can work in various settings or for herself, Olympia is also able to schedule her days as she likes, or as her family responsibilities require. "The planning I did when I chose my career has paid off in many ways," she says now. "Sometimes people tell me how lucky I am to be able to have both a family and a well-paying job, but I know that luck had very little to do with it."

What Olympia realized, and what more and more parents are coming to realize, is that time plays a crucial role in our lives. Everyone would like to have a wonderful career and a terrific marriage, perfect children, tons of friends, and a full social life. But all these things take time. If you need to spend 40 hours a week just to make enough money to get by, you will need to make trade-offs. You will have to sacrifice in some other areas of your life.

It might be difficult to imagine what a day would be like as a working mother. In the circle below, Olympia has drawn a circle graph of her typical work day (four hours per day).

Olympia's
Time Circle

noon
1
2
4
6 pm
7
10
midnight
6 am
7
8
9
In office
Personal time
Pick up baby /errands
Family time
Personal time /office catchup
Sleep
Care for baby
Ready for work
Baby to sitters

In the blank circle that follows, try to draw a graph of what the work day would be like for Barbara or another young mother who has an infant but still needs to work full time (eight hours per day).

Barbara's
Time Circle

noon
6 am
6 pm
midnight

Time and the Single Parent

Vicki's Story

Now that Vicki is a single parent, time is her most precious commodity. Her two children are too young to be of help around the house, so Vicki is responsible for everything from taking care of the kids to mowing the lawn, fixing the car, making the meals—and making the money. Draw a chart below showing what a typical day might be like for Vicki. Assume that she works full time, and that there's no one she can count on to take care of any of the household chores.

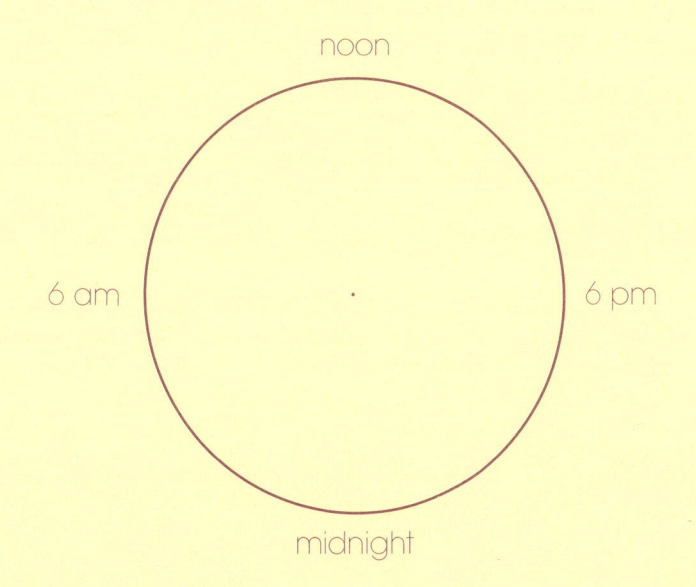

noon

6 am   6 pm

midnight

Time Is Money

As Olympia's story shows, if you choose a career that pays well enough, you have more options. You will probably have to work harder at first to prove that you are good at your job and committed to it. But then you can make many of your own decisions. Do you want to work part time? Do you want to start a business of your own? In many low-paying jobs, your time is really *their* time. But if you plan well, it can be all your time—and your money.

Compare the average hourly salaries of some careers listed below. What relationship do you see between salary and freedom to combine career and family or to pursue other interests?

AVERAGE HOURLY SALARIES*

Secretary	$ 7.21
Certified public accountant	$ 15.00
Store clerk	$ 4.50
Computer service technician	$ 14.00
Registered nurse	$ 11.54
Physician	$ 42.79
Elementary school teacher	$ 9.86
Psychologist (Ph.D.)	$ 21.63
Switchboard operator	$ 5.75
Civil engineer	$ 16.83
Newspaper reporter	$ 9.61
Auto mechanic	$ 13.02
Bank teller	$ 4.18
Electrician	$ 17.12
Hotel room attendant	$ 5.24
Computer systems analyst	$ 14.71
Typist	$ 6.59
House and construction painter	$ 16.14
Dental technician	$ 5.67
Optician	$ 12.01
Police officer	$ 12.50
Podiatrist	$ 12.03
Receptionist	$ 5.04

A secretary working **eight** hours makes $_____ a day.

A certified public accountant working **four** hours makes $_____ a day.

A shop clerk working **eight** hours makes $_____ a day.

A computer service technician working **four** hours makes $_____ a day.

A registered nurse working **eight** hours makes $_____ a day.

A physician working **four** hours makes $_____ a day.

An elementary teacher working **eight** hours makes $_____ a day.

A psychologist (Ph.D.) working **four** hours makes $_____ a day.

A switchboard operator working **eight** hours makes $_____ a day.

A civil engineer working **four** hours makes $_____ a day.

A newspaper reporter working **eight** hours makes $_____ a day.

An auto mechanic working **four** hours makes $_____ a day.

A bank teller working **eight** hours makes $_____ a day.

An electrician working **four** hours makes $_____ a day.

A hotel room attendant working **eight** hours makes $_____ a day.

A computer systems analyst working **four** hours makes $_____ a day.

A typist working **eight** hours makes $_____ a day.

A house painter working **four** hours makes $_____ a day.

A dental technician working **eight** hours makes $_____ a day.

An optician working **four** hours makes $_____ a day.

A police officer working **eight** hours makes $_____ a day.

A podiatrist working **four** hours makes $_____ a day.

A receptionist working **eight** hours makes $_____ a day.

*About the salary figures in this book:
The salaries reported in this book are those reported by the Bureau of Labor Statistics and/or by professional associations. They are national averages (for both men and women) that will vary in different parts of the country. They do not represent the lowest or the highest salaries for each category. The authors recommend you consult a copy of *The American Almanac of Jobs and Salaries* by John W. Wright for a more in-depth salary review.

Complete the bar graph below to show the average daily salaries of, first, the eight hour day positions and then the four hour day positions.

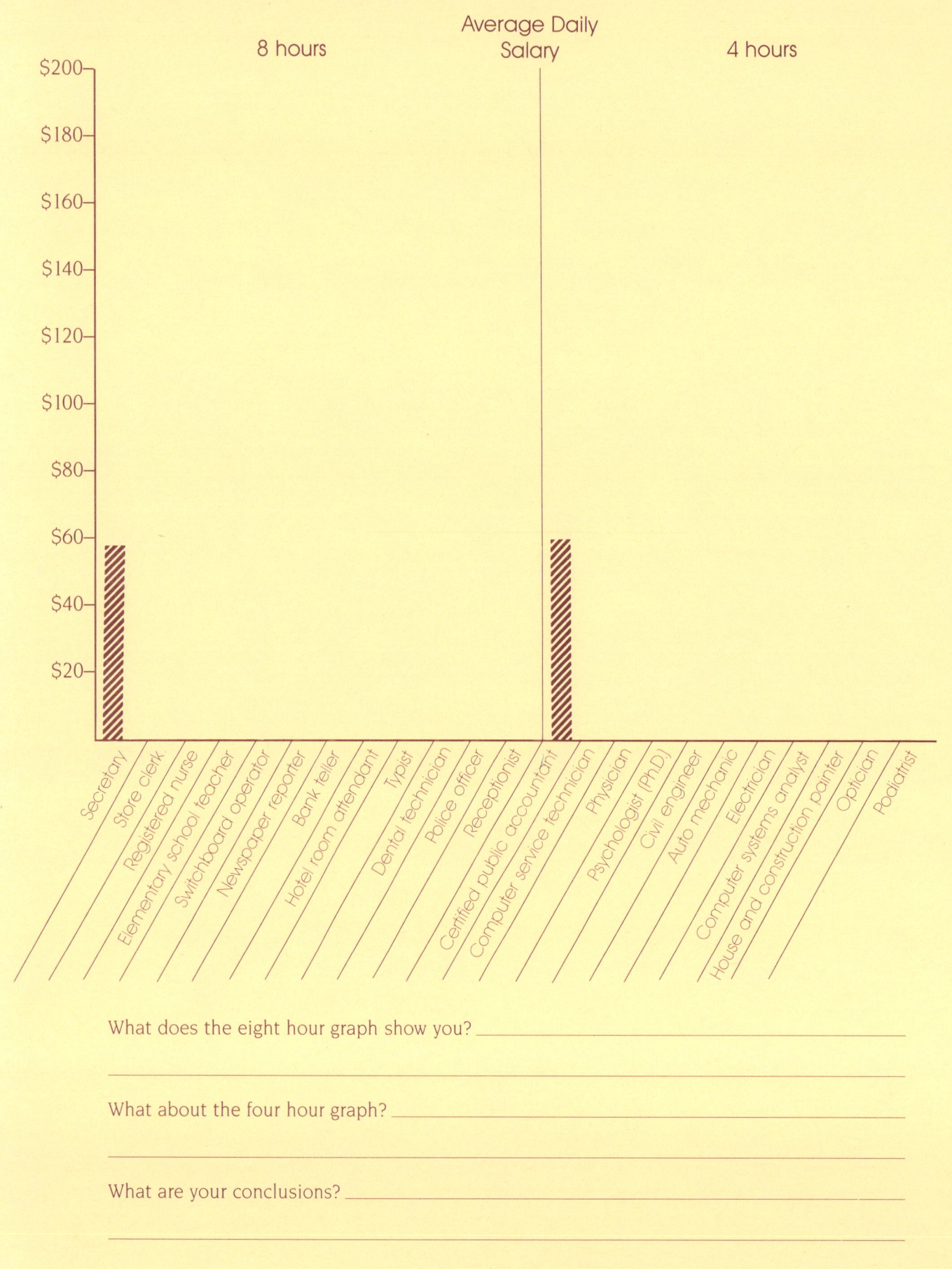

Average Daily Salary

8 hours | 4 hours

[Bar graph with y-axis from $20 to $200 in increments of $20. X-axis labels (diagonal): Secretary, Store clerk, Registered nurse, Elementary school teacher, Switchboard operator, Newspaper reporter, Bank teller, Hotel room attendant, Typist, Dental technician, Police officer, Receptionist, Certified public accountant, Computer service technician, Physician, Psychologist (PhD), Civil engineer, Auto mechanic, Electrician, Computer systems analyst, House and construction painter, Optician, Podiatrist. Two bars drawn at approximately $58-$60, one on the 8-hour side (Secretary) and one on the 4-hour side (Certified public accountant).]

What does the eight hour graph show you? _____

_____

What about the four hour graph? _____

_____

What are your conclusions? _____

_____

70

Remember Vicki, the single parent? Every hour she spends at a paying job is an hour away from home and children. If she could make enough money to support her family at a part-time job, life would be much less frantic. Turn back to the career chart on page 69.

In which jobs might Vicki be able to live on the earnings from a four hour work day?

_____   _____   _____

_____   _____   _____

Which jobs would require her to work a full eight hours in order to exist above the poverty line?

_____   _____   _____

_____   _____   _____

Are there some jobs that would not provide enough to live on for an adult and two children *even* working 40 hours a week? Which ones are they?

_____   _____   _____

_____   _____   _____

With a high-paying job, a woman can be assured that her family will be provided for even if she is its sole support, and even if she can only work part-time. If a woman has not prepared herself for a career with education and experience, however, she may find few job openings that pay more than clerking in a store. The only option she has then is to work overtime or take a second job.

What happens to her time chart if she needs to work overtime or take on a second job to make ends meet? Draw the time chart of a woman with two children who works 9 to 5 in the local shopping mall and then babysits in the evening for her neighbor's infant.

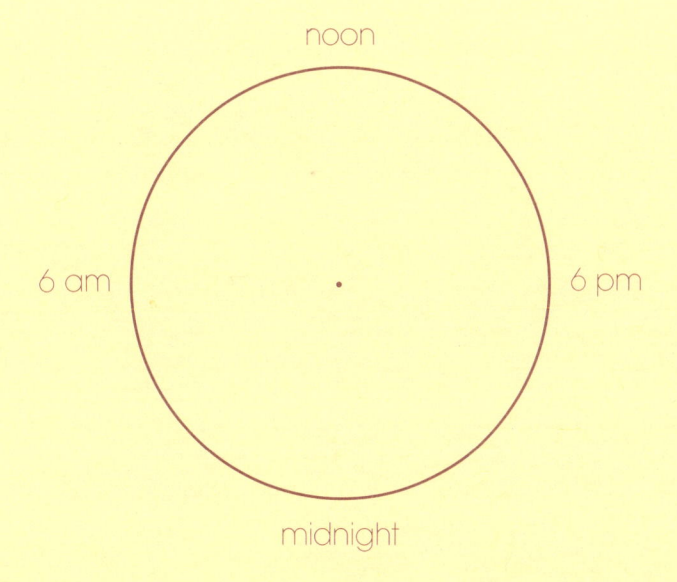

noon

6 am   6 pm

midnight

71

Louann's Story

Louann wasn't sure whether she wanted to be a science teacher or a pharmacist. She knew it would take her two years longer to become a licensed pharmacist, and she thought it would be more enjoyable to work with children. Louann told her school counselor that she was leaning toward the teaching career. Miss Jones asked Louann if she was planning to have children of her own. "Oh, certainly. My children will be the most important thing in my life," Louann replied. "But I guess I'd still have to work and I think my work will be important to me." Miss Jones took out a list of salary levels for different professionals. "Well," she said, "as a teacher, you would probably have to work full time. The salary levels are much lower, and there really aren't many opportunities for part-time jobs. I know many young women go into teaching because, while their children are young, the work schedule is convenient. That's true, but flexibility and pay are not what they might be. Pharmacists, on the other hand, make more money per hour worked. And there are lots of part-time jobs. It might be worth the additional education in order to have a higher salary and more flexible hours when your children are young." Louann thought Miss Jones had a point. If she had to choose between two jobs that she would enjoy, she might as well go for the one that offered the opportunity to have the kind of family life she wanted. She could still work with children as a volunteer. She might even decide to change careers and become a science teacher when her own children were older.

Being a Parent is a Job, Too

If you were to believe what you see in some of the media, you would think that it's easy to combine a career and a family. There she is every time we turn on the TV or open a magazine: a beautifully dressed woman in an elegant home (in which not one stray toy or diaper bag can be seen), cradling a clean and smiling baby in one arm while closing a multi-million dollar deal over the phone and brushing off the advances of a Don Johnson look-alike who is persistently nibbling her neck. Well, why not! There may be a few women in the world who can carry this act off . . . very few.

For the rest of us, some compromises have to be made. Parents raising young children must devote thousands of hours to that all-important task. One study determined that, with a pre-schooler in the house, a parent needs to spend fifty to sixty hours a week on tasks related to housework and child care.[1] In other words, parenthood is more than a full-time (40 hour week) job. If you need to work outside the home to earn money as well, you are doubling the burden on yourself, your energy and your time. We are slowly learning ways to deal with the problems involved. Having a high-paying job with flexible hours seems to be one of the most workable solutions.

Below is a list of careers, some of which you may have considered for yourself. In which of these careers could you choose the hours you would like to work? Would you be able to work from 10 a.m. to 3 p.m. if those hours suited you best? If so circle the "Yes." Or would you most likely have someone else telling you when to work? If so circle the "No." How flexible is that career?

Most of the time:

Can a secretary choose her own hours?	Yes	No
Can a store clerk choose her own hours?	Yes	No
Can a nurse choose her own hours?	Yes	No
Can an elementary school teacher choose her own hours?	Yes	No
Can a bank teller choose her own hours?	Yes	No
Can a social worker choose her own hours?	Yes	No
Can an airline attendant choose her own hours?	Yes	No
Can a switchboard operator choose her own hours?	Yes	No
Can a file clerk choose her own hours?	Yes	No
Can a librarian choose her own hours?	Yes	No
Can a receptionist choose her own hours?	Yes	No
Can a dentist choose her own hours?	Yes	No
Can an architect choose her own hours?	Yes	No
Can a chiropractor choose her own hours?	Yes	No
Can a house painter choose her own hours?	Yes	No
Can an optometrist choose her own hours?	Yes	No
Can a physical therapist choose her own hours?	Yes	No
Can a photographer choose her own hours?	Yes	No
Can a psychologist choose her own hours?	Yes	No
Can an electrician choose her own hours?	Yes	No

What pattern do you see emerging from the responses above? _____
_____
_____

Do careers with flexible schedules usually require more preparation? More education? _____
_____

If the career you want to pursue is *not* flexible, can you foresee ways in which it might be made more so? Could you share the job with another person? Could you have a series of temporary jobs in this field? Are there ways in which employers or society could be encouraged to change? What could *you* do to encourage them?
_____
_____
_____
_____

The average annual salaries for the careers just discussed are listed below. Let's examine the difference in salaries between jobs with flexible hours and those without flexibility. In *pen* place a dot at the salary level of each career you identified as having flexible hours (a response of yes in the previous exercise). Connect these dots in pen. Now in *pencil* place a dot at the salary level of each career you identified as *not* having flexible hours (a response of no in the previous exercise). Connect these dots in pencil.

The pen graph represents careers with flexible hours and the pencil graph represents careers with inflexible hours.

Average Annual Salaries*

Social worker	$19,400	Airline attendant	$17,200
File clerk	$10,500	Librarian	$23,200
Chiropractor	$32,000	Optometrist	$45,000
Physical therapist	$42,000	Photographer	$29,000
Switchboard operator	$11,900	Receptionist	$10,500
Secretary	$15,000	Shop clerk	$9,400
Nurse	$24,000	Elementary teacher	$20,500
Bank teller	$8,700	Dentist	$65,900
Architect	$32,500	Psychologist (Ph.D.)	$45,000
House painter	$32,000	Electrician	$35,600

Salary axis (y-axis):
$75,000
$70,000
$65,000
$60,000
$55,000
$50,000
$45,000
$40,000
$35,000
$30,000
$25,000
$20,000
$15,000
$10,000
$ 5,000

Careers (x-axis): social worker, file clerk, chiropractor, physical therapist, switchboard operator, secretary, nurse, bank teller, architect, house painter, airline attendant, librarian, optometrist, photographer, receptionist, shop clerk, elementary teacher, dentist, psychologist (Ph.D), electrician

Which type of career generally pays more, a flexible or non-flexible career? _____

Can you explain the relationship between salary level and job flexibility? _____

Can you think of reasons why this relationship exists? (How much training is required? Has this job usually been held by more men in the past or more women?)

75

Jackie's and Marita's Story

As childhood friends, Jackie and Marita spent many long summer days building forts and working in Jackie's parents' tool shed. After high school graduation, both took courses at the community vocational school. Jackie became an independent contractor upon finishing her education, and Marita went to work for the phone company. Both were quite pleased with their jobs until, several years later, they began to raise families. Marita was able to take a month's maternity leave, but she wasn't assured that she would have the same job when she returned to work. Her first child had a chronic illness, but her supervisor warned her that continued absences to take care of her sick child would force the company to fire her. Marita didn't know which way to turn. She needed her job—but her young son needed her. Being a working mother was hard enough without all the stress her special situation was placing on her.

Jackie, on the other hand, was better able to set her own hours. Most of the people she worked for didn't care whether she arrived at 8 or 10 in the morning as long as their ceilings got patched or their walls got papered. When she became pregnant with her second child, Jackie didn't want to work around the paint fumes which were normally part of her work environment, so she decided to hire another woman to work with her. She was starting to put in too many hours, anyway, she thought. When she heard about Marita's difficulties, she asked her old friend to be her apprentice. The two are now partners in a very successful contracting business. They give each other the day off whenever a child is sick or has a birthday. And last year, when Marita's son Mark appeared as the lead carrot in his nursery school's production of "Peter Rabbit," the entire firm took the afternoon off to attend the gala opening performance.

What Jackie and Marita have, and what every working parent needs, is flexibility. So far, children have proved remarkably resistant to the idea that they must never throw up on Mommy's new suit when she bends down to kiss them good-bye in the morning, or that they should wait to gash a foot on a broken bottle until after 5 p.m. or, preferably, until the weekend. Flexibility lets you bend the rules that some people think are rigid as steel posts. Who says you have to work from 9 to 5? Who says you have to work 40 hours a week? When the world is changing as quickly as ours is today, it is important for people and jobs to be flexible. That is, we need to be able to adjust to changing conditions and changing needs in creative ways. If you can do that, you will not only survive, you will thrive, and so will the people around you.

Flexibility: An Important Career Characteristic

Unfortunately, the work world has not kept pace with the needs of women who now make up such a large portion of the workforce. More part-time and flex-time positions are available, but many employers are clinging to their old, rigid ways. Other employers view the choice to work part time as a part of their benefit package, and may pay employees who choose this benefit somewhat less than they pay their full-time workers. There is some validity in this argument, as it is more expensive for them to make these kinds of options available. Still, more changes need to be made, and in Chapter 12 we will talk about the ways you can help make them happen.

In the meantime, the most assured way to build flexibility into your career is to work for yourself. As your own boss, you have a unique view of both your own needs and the requirements of your career. You can use your good judgment to make the decisions which will lead to the most satisfying and successful life for you, your business and your family.

What kind of work can you do on your own? Professionals such as doctors, certified public accountants, dentists, financial planners, architects, and lawyers have great potential for success when they go into private practice. You will also want to consider being a consultant in your chosen field, using your skills on a freelance basis, going into sales, or starting your own business—being an entrepreneur like Jackie. Plumbers, mechanics, electricians, drafters and computer programmers are just a few of the people who can work for themselves. To make setting up your home-based business easier, there are now many good books on the topic.

Of course, hardly anyone can come right out of college and start working as a consultant or a freelancer. You will need to learn the "tricks of the trade" and educate yourself in every aspect of the business. This you will probably do in a "regular" job working for someone else. You may choose to stay there if you find that the position meets your needs. Obviously, all parents cannot—and do not want to—work for themselves. But by leaving that option open, you are putting yourself in the best position to make good decisions for your future. When you make your career choice, ask yourself some questions. How flexible is this choice? How do my plans for marriage and family fit? Does it allow for a sabbatical or leave of absence when I need time for parenting? Could I reduce my hours or my workload if I needed to? Could I learn new skills that would be transferable to other careers? You may want to consider some of the careers discussed in the next chapter.

REFLECTIONS

Chapter Five
Career Planning for Flexibility & Higher Salary

In the long run, people hit only what they aim at. Therefore, they had better aim at something high.

Opportunities are usually disguised as hard work, so most people don't recognize them.
—Ann Landers

According to the Bureau of Labor Statistics, the professional part-time workforce increased 50% between 1972 and 1982, and is still growing. Two and a third million people work part time in managerial and professional specialty occupations. The majority—71 percent—are women.

Professionals are at an advantage when it comes to working for themselves. Not surprisingly. They have already spent years preparing themselves to provide a service that is in demand. When a doctor opens a practice or a certified public accountant starts a firm, they are taking fewer risks than someone starting a restaurant or building a factory.

Professionals' investments are not in a product or a building, but in themselves. They have put time and energy into their education, and sacrificed years of earnings for the sake of their careers. But the lawyer, the doctor, the architect—all have special skills that cannot be taken away.

What are the careers we usually classify as professional? They include:

Law	Pharmacy	Certified Public Accounting
Dentistry	Medicine	Education
Engineering	Architecture	Veterinary medicine

Keep in mind that, within many of these professions, there are various specialties, and that some of them offer much more flexibility than others. You would probably have more flexibility as a dermatologist than as an emergency room doctor, for example. There is also a trend toward working in cooperative practices with sympathetic partners (who also want flexibility), a situation that can prove even more workable than establishing a solo practice.

These careers have more in common than the amount of flexibility they offer. All require some post-college training or education. All require high school and college math and/or science credits. And all make up for those requirements by offering attractive financial rewards. Average salaries are:

Career	Column 2 Average Annual Salary	Column 3 Average Half-time Salary	Column 4	
Lawyer	$52,000	_____	Yes	No
Dentist	$65,900	_____	Yes	No
Doctor	$89,000	_____	Yes	No
Pharmacist	$26,800	_____	Yes	No
Architect	$32,500	_____	Yes	No
Engineer	$35,000	_____	Yes	No
Certified public accountant	$31,500	_____	Yes	No
University professor	$32,000	_____	Yes	No
Veterinarian (federal)	$34,115	_____	Yes	No

Figure out how much money you could earn in each profession working only half-time, and enter that number in column 3.

Turn back to your sample budgets in Chapter 3 pages 44 to 46, and choose one you think you could live on comfortably with your two children. Enter that figure here

$_____.

Could you live comfortably working just half-time at any of the careers above? If so circle the "yes" in column 4. If not, circle the "no."

If you circled "yes," then it would be safe to assume that this profession could provide a decent living for you and your family if circumstances required that you support the family on your own income, or if you only wanted to work part time. And yet statistics show that only .6% of working women have jobs in these professions...less than 1% of all the women in the workforce.[1]

Suzuko's Story

After several years of attempting to balance her family life with a full-time job as a physician in a large medical center, Suzuko knew she needed a change. She found welcome relief as the fourth partner in a cooperative pediatrics clinic, where each of the doctors worked 25 hours a week. Since the other partners didn't have small children at home, they took the bulk of the emergency and after-hours calls, with the understanding that Suzuko would cover for them when they needed relief. There are times when Suzuko must work more than full time, but she and her family are much happier now that her hours are more flexible and she has more time at home.

Usually, we think of professionals as people totally committed to their careers. The re-runs on TV give no indication that Perry Mason or Dr. Kildare had any life outside the courtroom or operating room. But things have changed drastically in the past twenty years. The number of women entering the professions has meant more sensitivity to the other spheres of life. And this has been beneficial to professional men as well. Again, though, you must plan carefully and research your career choices well. There are still specialties within many professions that do not easily lend themselves to part-time or flexible work.

One thing is true:

The higher your present aspirations for educational and professional achievement, the more freedom you will have for parenting later in your life.

Free-lancer

The term "free-lance" comes from the days when knights and noblemen spent the better part of their time sticking swords through each other. Since there tended to be a lot of turnover among the knights aligned with each noble, the landowners began hiring "free lances," or knights who had allegiance to no one but themselves. A free-lance job is less dangerous today, and more popular than ever. Employers are looking for free-lancers in fields from computer programming to graphic design.

In fact, nearly any skill can be free-lanced—as long as you are good at what you do. Training is the obvious place to start, but you will probably also need practical experience to polish your talents and to give yourself credibility as a professional. As a free-lance writer, for example, you need a portfolio with samples of your work to show prospective clients. You might spend a few years working for a newspaper, magazine, or advertising agency in order to make a name for yourself and gather evidence of your abilities. (Hint: If you are considering a free-lance career, keep a sample of every kind of your work that you can. Even if you don't like the article about the German shepherd that does the imitation of a duck on roller-skates, it may be just the thing to convince someone else that you are the person for the job.)

Free-lancers often start their new careers while they are still working full time. It can take some time to build up a list of clients so, if you need a steady income, this is a good way to begin. The disadvantage is that, at first, you will be working at two jobs.

But, as a free-lancer, you will have a great deal of control over your time. You might be able to work full time when the kids are away at camp for two weeks, and, if you choose, you might not work at all when a situation at home demands your immediate attention. Or you might want to get up a 4 a.m. and put in three hours of work before the rest of the family awakens. You may earn more per hour than you would doing the same work as a permanent employee, since those who hire you do not have to provide any benefits beyond your fee. (This is one reason why your permanent employer might be willing to become your client when you start free-lancing. It also means that *you* will need to supply your own health insurance, pension plan, and so on—another disadvantage.) You will not necessarily become wealthy working this way. The big benefit is the freedom and flexibility you will receive.

In order to be successful, you need to be able to promote yourself and your business. You will not attract clients through mental telepathy. You must also be self-disciplined enough to do your work without external pressure. Meeting deadlines is an important part of the job. Organization and management skills are needed, since you will be responsible for getting the job, doing the job, and keeping a record of what you have done.

What kinds of skills can be free-lanced? The possibilities are endless. Free-lance jobs exist for writers, artists, musicians, word processors, mental and physical therapists, exercise trainers, dance instructors, carpenters, interior designers, wardrobe consultants, animal trainers, editors, key liners, upholsterers, furniture refinishers, tutors, and more.

Some examples of how it works:

A staff writer for a newspaper could free-lance writing books and articles.
A secretary could be a free-lance word processor.
A school teacher could be a free-lance tutor.
A professional musician could be a piano teacher.
A restaurant cook could become a caterer.
A hospital nurse could become an independent health care provider.

Can you think of possible free-lance opportunities for people in the following fields?

Sales clerk _____
_____

Graphic artist _____
_____

Police officer _____
_____

Airline pilot _____
_____

Professional athlete _____
_____

Groundskeeper _____
_____

Hotel maid _____
_____

Having some trouble? Well, a sales clerk with experience in selling clothing might be a wardrobe consultant or run a shopping service for professional people who don't have the time to shop. A graphic artist could design books, advertisements, or brochures. A police officer might be a security guard or a private detective. An airline pilot might give flying lessons or be available to pilot a corporate jet. A professional athlete could be a fitness instructor, or give lessons in tennis, skiing, or whatever. A groundskeeper might become a gardener or set up a lawn service. A hotel maid might make more money in less time as a private housekeeper. There are other possibilities, but you get the idea.

Sandy's Story

After earning a degree in journalism, Sandy spent several years working as a newspaper staff writer and then as an advertising copywriter. She began to write and sell magazine articles while still working full time. When she left her job, her former employer asked her to continue working on some of the accounts she was familiar with—at a higher hourly wage. That arrangement provided the financial security she needed while she set up her new career. After four years, Sandy earned more than she did at her full-time job, though she only worked about half the hours. She thought it was an ideal way to combine career and family.

Sales Person

Rosalie's Story

When a friend first suggested to Rosalie that she get a license to sell real estate, she laughed. "What does an elementary school teacher know about sales?" she thought. But, when she couldn't find a teaching position, Rosalie decided to give it a try. Getting the license was no problem. If there was one thing she knew, it was how to take a test. As she began her new career, she found that many of her teaching skills applied. She was still working with people, still diagnosing what their individual problems and needs were, and still trying to instill some enthusiasm for the product she had to offer. She usually did most of her work in the evening and on weekends when her husband was at home to take care of the children. Within two years, Rosalie was making about as much as she did as a teacher—having to be away from her family only half the amount of time.

Many people are very good at sales. And saleswork can be a terrific field for parents. It offers a chance for flexible hours, a chance for high pay, and a chance to be your own boss. And there is certainly no shortage of products! Look around. Just about everything you see was sold by someone. Besides real estate, you might consider selling insurance, securities, office equipment, computers, automobiles and so on. Keep in mind that some sales jobs require extensive travel. Steer away from those if you plan to have a family.

What kinds of sales positions do you think would interest you most? Make a list below.

_____   _____

_____   _____

_____   _____

_____   _____

_____   _____

People who are good at sales are generally able to speak effectively and persuasively. They are good listeners, and can also put their thoughts in writing. They are enthusiastic, and they have the ability to bounce back when, inevitably, they face rejection by a potential client. Ironically, sales has been considered a "man's job," although the description of the ideal salesperson fits a typical woman more than the average male. Studies show that more women than men are articulate, good listeners, people-oriented, intuitive (the ability to sense what other people are thinking or feeling), and persistent.

Sales positions are somewhat riskier than other high-paying, flexible jobs, since the best paid outside or independent salespersons work on a commission basis. (A commission is a percentage of the total amount of the sale. For example, a real estate agent usually gets 6% of the selling price of a house.) You don't get paid for putting in your hours, only for making sales. But great rewards are possible. If you want to put in the effort, there is, literally, no limit to the amount of money you can earn. Since there is a direct correlation between your income and your ability to sell, it's easy to measure how well you are doing. Another advantage of sales is that, in many cases, a college education or other specific training is not required.

Consultant

Fiona's Story

Fiona liked to make things work. Her employer soon learned that, when there was a problem in management, accounting, or program development, Fiona could be counted on to determine what was wrong and find a workable solution. When her firm began using computers for many of its operations, it was Fiona who set up the programs, taught her colleagues how to use them, and made sure that everything operated as efficiently as possible. As she completed this assignment, Fiona learned a great deal about designing computer programs to do specialized tasks and to meet individual needs. There was a high demand for a service like the one she could provide, so Fiona decided to become a consultant. That way, she could make use of her problem-solving talent and her specialized knowledge. She also appreciates the freedom and flexibility consulting provides.

Consulting is similar to free-lancing in that both usually involve short-term jobs for different employers. But while a free-lancer performs a specific task, a consultant sells advice by telling the employer what should be done to correct a problem or implement a new program. Even more than a free-lancer, a consultant needs to be a *recognized* expert in her field. That can mean years of training and experience in a position of high visibility before entering the consulting profession.

A consultant might be an expert in any number of fields. Today, technical expertise in areas like computer programming, business management, data base administration, systems analysis, telecommunications and office automation is particularly valuable. Consultants might also work in public relations, executive recruitment, or office efficiency. Or, on a smaller scale, there are color consultants, wardrobe consultants, and consultants to help you organize your closets or your life.

Whatever field you choose, you must constantly keep abreast of the latest trends and information in your specialty, or you will soon find yourself without clients. Becoming—and remaining—an expert in your field takes time and energy, but it is absolutely essential. Consultants also need to be able to promote themselves, and to seek out new clients. They should be able to work well with people, since their work requires a good deal of negotiation, persuasion and education.

If you like to diagnose problems, and to recommend and implement solutions to them, then you might keep consulting in mind. This is an area that, in time, offers high salary and flexibility. It's common for consultants in many fields to earn $20,000 to $30,000 per year for less than full-time work. For well-known consultants in a high-demand area, personal earnings of $100,000 to $200,000 are not uncommon.

As a consultant, you are in a good position when you decide it's time to start a family. But, since you need training and experience in your field of expertise and also need to be well-known, it's likely that you will have to delay parenthood until you are over 30.

Would you make a good consultant? Are you:

Yes No
☐   ☐   Inquisitive?
☐   ☐   A problem solver?
☐   ☐   A good communicator?
☐   ☐   Well-organized?
☐   ☐   Tactful and cooperative?
☐   ☐   Persuasive?
☐   ☐   Logical?
☐   ☐   Self-directed?
☐   ☐   Empathetic (able to know how the other person feels)?
☐   ☐   Willing to take risks?
☐   ☐   Confident of your skills?
☐   ☐   A self-promoter?

If you answered "yes" to at least eight of the items above, you might think about adding "consultant" to your list of potential future careers.

If you do become a consultant, you might also consider branching out to give seminars on the topics of your expertise. Some day, you may want to write a book about the things you know best. It's a good way to pass on valuable information to many more people while firmly establishing your own expertise and enhancing your income.

Manager

Pearl's Story

After earning her MBA (Master's degree in Business Administration) from a prestigious business school, Pearl went to work for a large corporation. For eight years, she traveled extensively, worked nearly every evening, and most weekends, as well. By the time she and her husband, Ted, had their first child, Pearl was vice-president in charge of marketing. She wasn't able to be away from her job for more than a month, but she and Ted hired a live-in housekeeper to help care for their new daughter. Pearl would have liked to have had more time at home, but her hours were somewhat flexible, and at least she knew that her baby was well taken care of. "I love my child *and* my job," she says. "But it's impossible to be in two places at once. I decided I would just have to do my best, and not worry about the things I couldn't do."

Let's face it. Few corporations are interested in free-lance, part-time or consulting managers. Most managers work a forty-plus hour week. It is not unusual to put in extensive overtime when travel is necessary or an important deadline must be met. Still, once you become a manager, you may be in a better position to become a parent, as well. In most companies, executives have much more freedom to set their own hours than, say, their secretaries do. If they take off early one afternoon to see a school play or a little league game, they may have to put in some evening hours, but they can do that according to their own schedule.

Corporate executives make enough money to be able to hire household help. They may also have more vacation time. And the experience they are acquiring will be valuable in other pursuits, if they decide to leave the corporate environment. Consider, too, that the opposite situation often occurs: People who have gained experience and proved their value in fields like child care or travel arrangement might find employment within a corporation when their expertise is needed.

Good managers seem to share certain traits. It goes without saying that they are experts in their field. They can make considered decisions quickly. They can motivate other people to do their best work. And they are not afraid to take a well-calculated risk now and again. Are you one of these people? Could you be?

EVALUATE YOURSELF

To help decide if you have management potential, consider the following statements. Indicate whether they are "very true," "sometimes true," "not true," or if you are "undecided" by putting a mark in the appropriate column.

	Very True	Sometimes True	Not True	Undecided
When people are counting on me, I don't let them down.				
I can take and give directions well.				
I am a team player.				
I try to be consistent without being inflexible.				
I manage my time well enough to meet my deadlines.				
I am self-directed. No one has to push me to do my work.				
I communicate well verbally and in writing.				
I can be assertive without being aggressive or abrasive.				
I have the enthusiasm needed to motivate others.				
I have enough confidence to delegate responsibility to others.				
I can set priorities for myself and for others.				
I can make considered decisions quickly.				
I can persuade and negotiate with others to get what I want.				
I am happy to work for future rewards rather than immediate gratification.				

If most of your responses are in the first two columns, management should be one area you consider when researching career opportunities.

Of course, it's not easy. Managers put in extra hours just as a matter of course. They work harder than their subordinates. It's no wonder they are also prone to stress, illnesses and all the accompanying side effects. Even if you are lucky enough to have a part-time management position, it is understood that you may have to work many additional hours during emergencies and that you will get phone calls at home. With more power comes more responsibility.

As more women enter the realm of management and become policy makers within the organization, they may be able to make changes which will make it easier for all employees to balance career and family responsibilities. The working world was created by men, for men with traditional male values. This philosophy creates problems for parents who give equal priority to their careers and their families. To many supervisors, part-time work is a sign of not being committed, not taking the job seriously enough, or simply of laziness. Employers still reward those who work long hours. In order to do that, and to be a parent at the same time, you must have strong support systems.

Rigid policies are becoming obsolete in some companies. Flexibility is now seen as a strategic tool for achieving top production and performance. We will discuss some of these topics in Chapter 12.

Entrepreneur

About three million American women now own and operate their own businesses. The number of women entrepreneurs increased 37 percent from 1977 to 1985, while their male counterparts increased their numbers by just 10 percent. These are not really surprising statistics. Corporate America has not reacted as quickly as it might to the needs of its female employees. And women, especially, have been disillusioned by what traditional careers have to offer. Most of these jobs do not readily adjust to the requirements of parents of young children.

In the early years of entrepreneurship, there will probably not be time for family responsibilities either. But once established in your own business, you will be able to make your own rules. If you are willing to trade a few years of stress, risk and just plain hard work for a more rewarding and flexible future, entrepreneurship may be for you.

In the past, it often took a small fortune just to *become* an entrepreneur: You usually needed to build a factory and buy a lot of equipment. With the advent of our service and information society, all that has changed. You might need nothing more than a desk, a phone, and some stationery to set up a soon-to-be-thriving business. Entrepreneurs are succeeding with such businesses as answering services, catering, party planning, word processing, and personal shopping. You can take your plan as far as your imagination allows as long as you are willing to work hard. The value of your enterprise comes from your own knowledge, creativity, and energy.

Wendy's Story

It seemed that Wendy was a born entrepreneur. Like many children, she started a lemonade stand when she was eight. Unlike most children, however, she used the money she made during her first weekend of business to a) hire other children to do the selling and b) buy more lemons and sugar—in other words, to expand. Two years later, Wendy went into the coupon/shopping business. She clipped coupons from magazines and newspapers, and talked her mother into letting her do the grocery shopping. In return for her time, Wendy could keep all the money she saved by using coupons. Soon Wendy was working for friends of the family as well and, thanks to those glorious "double coupons," she made between eight and ten dollars an hour at her job. Not bad for a ten-year-old! In high school, Wendy set up a personal errand service. She hired her friends to run errands for busy families in the area, did the billing, and kept a commission for herself. Today, Wendy, at 30, employs 45 people in her personalized shopping service. She recently told an interviewer she became an entrepreneur because, "I have always wanted to work for myself and to be *in control* of my life. I have a dream and I'm willing to work hard enough to make it come true."

Entrepreneurs usually make a conscious choice to go into business for themselves after spending time in a large corporation and finding the rules too rigid and the opportunities too limited. They believe they have a better way of doing something, and they want to be compensated for their efforts. Today, a surprising number of new businesses are owned and run by women. They have their problems, but many entrepreneurial women feel they have greater control of their lives and their time when they work for themselves.

Benefits include:

- Being your own boss, deciding when you will work, and how hard.
- Being financially rewarded for the results you achieve.
- Having more control over your time and your life.
- Being able to offer a less rigid environment for your own employees.
- Being better able to be available when your children need you.
- Making more money (if the business succeeds).
- Gaining self-esteem as you watch your business do well.

Disadvantages for entrepreneurs include:

- Often taking larger personal and financial risks.
- Needing to get your training and experience in business management before you can begin your own business.
- Delaying marriage and/or childbirth until you are established.
- Working long hours until your business is established (at which point you will have more flexibility).

The following personal evaluation will help you assess whether entrepreneurship should be something you consider in your career search.

ENTREPRENEURIAL CHECKLIST

Select the answer which best describes, or comes closest to your feelings.

Willingness to risk money:
- [ ] 1. As long as I feel that there is a good chance of success, I'll go for it without hesitation.
- [ ] 2. I'm willing to invest some money, but I always want to leave a sizable cushion, just in case.
- [ ] 3. I have never really felt comfortable risking money or time on things I'm not absolutely sure of.

Independence:
- [ ] 1. Most of all, I want to be my own boss; it's my major goal.
- [ ] 2. I don't mind working for other people, but I'd rather be on my own.
- [ ] 3. Being on my own really scares me. I'd rather have the security of being an employee, and let someone else worry about the problems.

Flexibility:
- [ ] 1. I adapt to change quickly and decisively.
- [ ] 2. I move, but it takes time and careful consideration.
- [ ] 3. I would rather see things stay the same; I get uptight when change occurs.

Self-Confidence:
- [ ] 1. I am very confident in myself and know that I can handle most situations.
- [ ] 2. I am confident most of the time, particularly when I know the ground rules.
- [ ] 3. I'm not in control of my destiny; other people really control my future.

Attitude toward people:
- [ ] 1. I am naturally drawn to people; I like them, and they like me.
- [ ] 2. I find most people enjoyable, and most people are attracted to me.
- [ ] 3. I like things more than people and don't have many friends.

Knowledge of the particular business:
- [ ] 1. I know the business that I've been thinking about well and will enjoy it.
- [ ] 2. I'm reasonably confident I can learn the business, and it appears that I will enjoy it.
- [ ] 3. I am not familiar with this type of business, nor do I know whether I will enjoy it.

Ability to start from scratch:
- [ ] 1. I enjoy the challenge of building something from scratch on my own; I'm a self-starter.
- [ ] 2. If given basic guidelines, I can do a good job.
- [ ] 3. I really prefer to have the entire job laid out; then I'll do it well.

Commitment:
- [ ] 1. I have a high drive and commitment, and won't stop until the project is done.
- [ ] 2. I seem to have a high level of perseverance when things are going well.
- [ ] 3. I start many projects, but rarely find time to finish them.

Common sense:
- [ ] 1. I consider myself realistic, and "street wise" when it comes to business.
- [ ] 2. Most business situations make sense, but there are areas where I feel out of step.
- [ ] 3. I am inexperienced and impractical in business matters.

Willingness to accept failure:
- [ ] 1. "Nothing ventured, nothing gained" is my motto.
- [ ] 2. I want to succeed, but if I fail, I will accept it.
- [ ] 3. I want to avoid failure, and won't take a risk if it doesn't look like a sure thing.

Health:
- [ ] 1. I have excellent health and feel good, both physically and mentally.
- [ ] 2. I get sick on occasion, but it doesn't last long.
- [ ] 3. I have problems with my health; illness always seems to get in my way.

Work habits:
- [ ] 1. I plan before I start and then work my plan; I'm well-organized.
- [ ] 2. I find that I'm organized most of the time; but on occasion, I do get out of control.
- [ ] 3. I take things as they come, and sometimes get priorities confused.

This checklist is for self evaluation of your personal characteristics, to see if you will have a better-than-average chance of success as an entrepreneur. The material may touch on some tender personal areas; you'll have to be honest with yourself. Be careful to avoid self deception; don't brush the negatives under the rug.

To total your score, add up all the checked numbers. A number one has the weight of one, a number two scores a two and a three equals three. If your total score is between 12 and 16, you are a good candidate and should consider starting your own business at some time.

This short personal appraisal is by no means an evaluation of whether you are qualified to be an entrepreneur. It is simply a way of focusing on your personal attributes, and it may help you decide on taking that major step. You may want to ask a few of your close friends or relatives to evaluate you. Their viewpoint may provide a more objective evaluation than that which you could do on your own.

Reprinted with permission: *How To Start, Expand And Sell A Business, A Complete Guidebook for Entrepreneurs*, by James C. Comiskey.

Daniel's Story

When Daniel devised a way to make double fudge chocolate chip brownies with just 25 calories per enormous serving, word got around. He could have sold his recipe for thousands of dollars, but he decided to market the product himself. Today, Daniel's Diet Brownies are sold in every major city in the world. He travels constantly to oversee his entrepreneurial empire, often appears on TV talk shows, and has recently contracted to write his life story. He hasn't found time to marry and have children yet, but he hasn't had time to worry about it, either.

As Wendy's and Daniel's stories illustrate, you can be an entrepreneur on many different levels and in just about any field. Some people are happy with a small local business (maybe a boutique or a catering service) that permits them to have time for family, friends and outside interests. Others want to see how successful they can be, and are willing to invest the time necessary to build a business known nationally, or even internationally. Either way, entrepreneurship can be an excellent way for men and women to take control of their lives.

What If You Think You're Shy?

Don't dismiss the career fields we've discussed here just because you think you are too shy to promote yourself or your business. It's not necessary to be the stereotypical back-slapping, joke-telling personality to make a sale or gain a client's trust. You may not be comfortable in some kinds of sales positions, but there is no reason you can't be successful in any field that appeals to you, any field you're good at and are willing to work at. As Fiona discovered, if your service is needed and there are few people who can deliver it as well as you, your business will grow by word of mouth. You will also find that, as you gain experience and education, your confidence level will grow (more about this in the next chapter). If you want to feel more comfortable in your position, there are self-development courses and seminars offered throughout the country. With education, training and practice, you can learn to feel more at ease. Remember, too, that you don't have to do all promotion in person, by yourself. You might hire someone to write brochures or news releases about your business. (Or you might find that you're less shy on paper, and write them yourself.) Or you might team up with a partner who is more at ease in the public arena and can promote the business but, perhaps, lacks some of your technical or creative skills.

The Technological Age—The Great Equalizer

As we've said before, our society is becoming less industrial, and increasingly more centered around information, communication and technology. The computer is the center of this new age.

Many women are finding, to their delight and surprise, that they can do much better in jobs with new technology firms than they ever could in the traditional corporate environment. There are several reasons why this may be true.

> **First,** most of these new companies are run by younger people who did not grow up with the same feelings about women in the workplace that older corporate executives so often have. They have fewer stereotypes about women, and are more willing to judge them on their job performance rather than their sex.
>
> **Second,** the jobs themselves have not been around long enough to have a sex-typed connotation. When someone says "secretary" most people still think of a woman, but when someone says "computer programmer" or "computer technician" we have a much fuzzier picture of the sex of the worker involved. This fact gives women greater access to any kind of position they are capable of filling.

Remember, too, that technology now affects nearly every job category. Whether you are a sales clerk at Sears, or president of the company, you need to know how to use a computer.

Consider the following careers. What kind of technical background or ability is needed in these fields today? How has technology made these jobs easier or more enjoyable? Write your answers in column 1.

Now, be imaginative. Look into the future. Pretend you are the director of product development for a large international computer company. You have been asked to write a report that gives some ideas for creative innovations that the company might develop. How might computers or robotics have changed these jobs by the year 2000? Write down your ideas in column 2.

	Column 1	Column 2
Manager		
Homemaker		
Court reporter		
Nurse		
School teacher		
Store clerk		
Receptionist		
Newspaper reporter		
Graphic artist		
Architect		
Pharmacist		
Police officer		

Was that fun or easy for you? If so, you might have the kind of creative talent that will take you far! Look into one of the careers in technology. It's a new world!

Note: Just a few years ago, women were being urged *not* to learn how to type—many people thought that ability would only keep women in secretarial positions. Today, however, everyone needs this skill. Only now we call it keyboarding. So if most of your time is spent behind a typewriter today, you've got a head start. Why not get the training you need and graduate to computers...higher salary, more flexibility.

If You're Not Going to College

Gloria's Story

Gloria enlisted in the Navy after high school because it offered training possibilities, travel and excellent benefits. Gloria liked it so much, she decided to make the military her career. She was able to retire at age 38, after 20 years of service, and received 50% of her base pay as a pension. At this time her children were two and four years old. Because she had a strategic plan, she was able to become a full-time wife and mother. Later, she thought, she would start a new career as a technical writer, but for the present she was glad she could devote her time and energy to her family.

Wesley's Story

Wesley wanted a good job, one that would allow him to be a responsible parent—but he didn't want to go to college. After doing some research, he decided to become a court reporter. The law had always fascinated him, and he liked the atmosphere of the courtroom. Wesley enjoyed detail work, and court reporting entailed lots of it. He could learn the skills he needed in about two years, and his entry level salary would be about $25,000. Another thing Wesley liked was the fact that court reporters can work free-lance, putting in as little or as much time as they like.

It isn't necessary to have four or eight years of post high school education to make a good living. There are plenty of good jobs requiring only two years of post high school training. Also, the U.S. Department of Labor predicts that competition for jobs requiring a college degree will increase during this decade. Up to 25 percent of college graduates may end up in jobs that don't require a baccalaureate degree.

Advantages of these non-college careers can include:
- Shorter preparation time
- The opportunity to earn money for college
- Union contracts guaranteeing wage levels, time off, etc.
- Less delay necessary for marriage and parenting
- Less time necessary to become established in the field
- Often more satisfaction for people who like to work with their hands

Possible disadvantages might be:
- Physically more exhausting than a sedentary career
- Lower status, if that is a concern to you
- Two incomes often required to buy a house

It is possible to find many jobs that combine a reasonably high salary, some flexibility (especially in the free-lance areas) and require two years or less of training.

Some jobs to consider along these lines are:

- Photographer
- Insurance salesperson
- Real estate salesperson
- Carpenter
- Caterer
- Computer systems technician
- Court reporter
- Dispensing optician
- Electronic equipment service technician
- Painter
- Paper hanger
- Detective
- Printer and lithographer
- Graphic artist
- Technical writer
- Word processor
- Sales representative
- Electrician
- Auctioneer
- Florist
- Air traffic controller
- Wedding consultant
- Horse trainer
- Actress/actor
- Dancer
- Rock musician
- Agent
- Model
- Truck driver
- Contractor
- Blacksmith
- Jockey
- Golf pro
- Travel agent
- Farmer/rancher
- Real estate developer
- Gardener
- Welder

Every calling is great when greatly pursued.
—Oliver Wendell Holmes, Jr.

REFLECTIONS

One can never consent to creep
when one feels an impulse to soar.
—Helen Keller

Nothing in life is to be feared. It is only
to be understood.
—Marie Curie

Chapter Six

Why Do We Choose What We Choose?

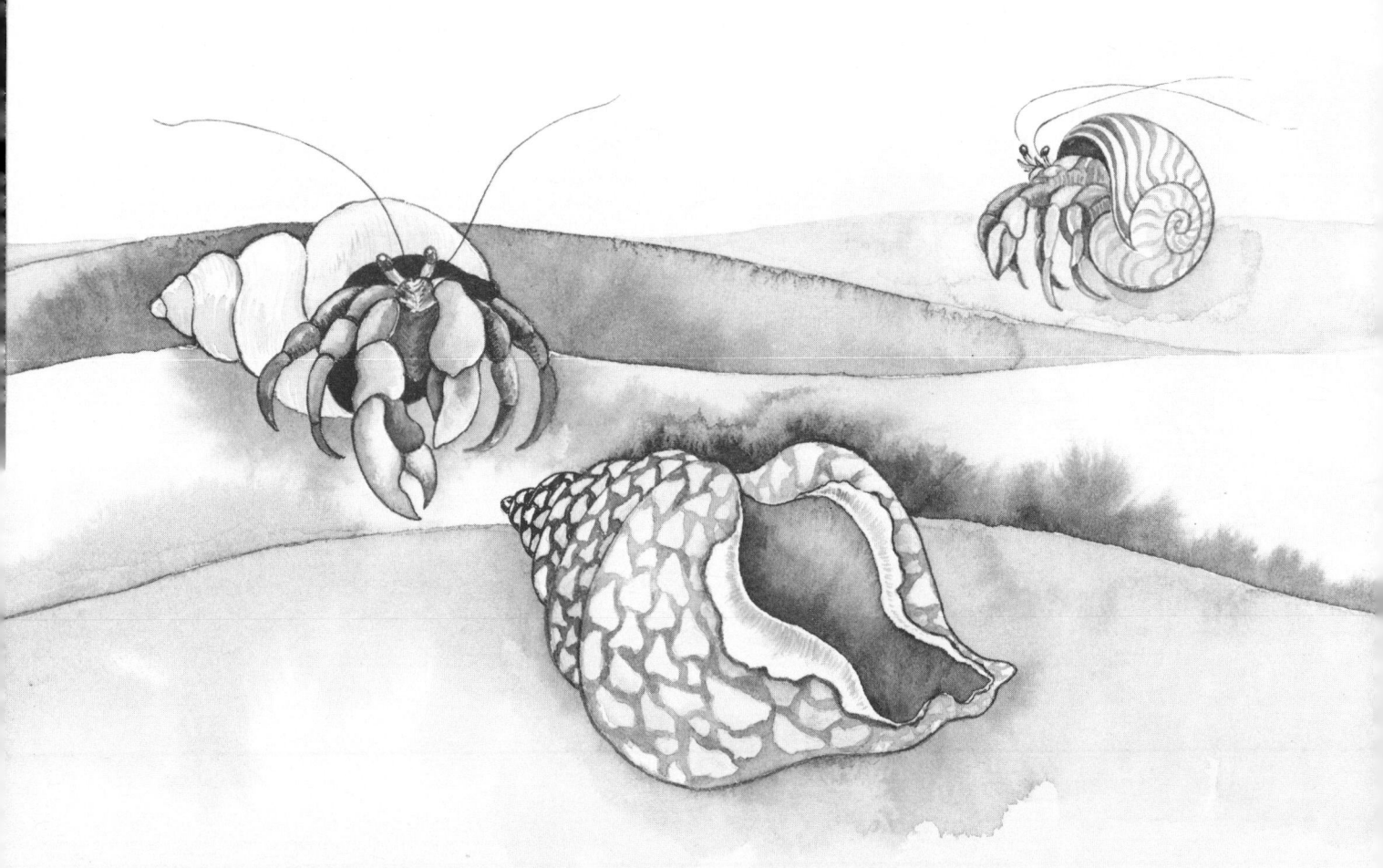

Bif & Muffy's Story

Bif and Muffy were twins. Their parents loved them both, and tried to raise them by the same rules. Yet it wasn't long before subtle differences in their interests and behavior began to emerge. Bif was a more active child than his sister, and their parents seemed to expect that of him. Muffy, on the other hand, could count on being praised for her ability to tell stories and her knack for getting along with the rest of the kids. When they started school, Bif's ability to throw a ball farther than even some of the second graders made him an immediate hit on the playground. Muffy's fame came from her prowess with a jump rope. As they grew up, their interests became even more diverse. Maybe this had something to do with what they saw on TV, or what their teachers and friends thought and did. Maybe there was a relationship between the twins' interests and those of their parents. (Their father, Tip, was a football coach, and their mom, Flopsy, worked in a boutique.) Bif entered college as a pre-dental student; Muffy wanted to teach pre-school. Today, Bif has a successful dental practice. Muffy has been struggling to support herself and her own set of twins, Peter and Bunny, since her marriage broke up three years ago. "Sometimes," Muffy says today, "I compare my life to my brother's, and wonder how the two of us ended up in such very different places."

For years it was assumed that a person's fate was determined at birth—if you were born male, you could expect certain things from life; if you were born female, your life would be much different. Blacks were expected to have different aspirations than whites, and people born without a great deal of money were encouraged to "stay in their place."

Today we know that our futures have more to do with the choices we make than with our biological makeup or where we were born. But there are forces at work in the world that influence those choices. Parents, friends, teachers and society at large still tend to encourage girls to think and behave in one way, and boys in another. All too often, distinctions are made on the basis of race or income rather than intelligence or ambition. Because white young men are expected to have higher career aspirations, they are more likely to excel in high school math and science classes, and they make up a majority of the students in college professional programs requiring math, science and technology. This is one reason (there are many others) why men make more money than women, and whites usually make more money than minorities. In this chapter, we will examine some of the forces that lead us to choose what we choose.

The Wage Gap Quiz

It is common knowledge that women earn less than men in our society. But how familiar are you with the specific facts and figures relating to this issue?

1. In 1984 the median full-time income for all men was $23,218 while for all women the average full-time salary was
    a. $24,353.
    b. $20,315.
    c. $16,989.
    d. $14,479.

2. There are more than 500 different job categories from which to choose a career. Nearly one-third of all working women are concentrated in _____ of those categories.
    a. 180
    b. 93
    c. 28
    d. 9

3. Women workers with four or more years of college have an average income only slightly above men who have
    a. one to three years of high school
    b. a high school degree
    c. two years of college
    d. four or more years of college

4. In 1981 women constituted _____% of the skilled craft and kindred workers.
    a. 46.1%
    b. 18.2%
    c. 6.3%
    d. 3.3%

5. Women carpenters were _____% of all carpenters in 1981.
    a. 25%
    b. 18%
    c. 10%
    d. 2%

6. Of the 500 fastest-growing private companies in America, as related by **INC.** magazine, _____% are run by women.
    a. 33%
    b. 20%
    c. 12%
    d. 4%

7. The average net worth of a man running one of the "INC. 500" companies is $4.8 million while the average net worth of a woman running an "INC. 500" company is
    a. $1.6 million.
    b. $2.2 million.
    c. $4 million.
    d. $5.2 million.

8. _____% of working women earn more than $20,000 per year.
    a. 55%
    b. 30%
    c. 10%
    d. 5%

9. _____% of employed women in the United States work in managerial positions.
    a. 3%
    b. 7%
    c. 24%
    d. 36%

10. In 1984, one out of every _____ women earned less than $10,000 per year when working full time.
    a. 20
    b. 14
    c. 9
    d. 4

11. In 1960 women in managerial positions earned 58% of the male wage; in 1980 they earned _____
    a. 86%
    b. 74%
    c. 55%
    d. 38%

Answers follow.

107

ANSWERS

1. In 1984, the median full-time income for all men was $23,218 while for all women the average full-time salary was

   (d) $14,479.[1] The gap exists in nearly all job categories. Male lawyers make more than female lawyers with the same amount of experience. Male bus drivers make more than female bus drivers. And male managers make more than female managers. The gap is narrower, however, when you compare men and women in the same profession than it is when you compare the salaries of men and women in general. This difference is in large part due to the fact that the work women do has not been valued and there are more men than women in the jobs offering the highest pay. Women are free to choose these professions, too, and more women are making that choice, while other women work to raise the status and pay of "women's professions."

2. There are more than 500 different job categories from which to choose a career. Nearly one-third of all working women are concentrated in

   (d) 9 of these categories.[2] And most of the total number of workers in these categories are women. The overwhelming majority of clerical and secretarial workers, cashiers and sales persons, waitresses, nurses and elementary school teachers are women. Although some of these categories require a college degree, they do not offer high salaries. Some people believe that jobs requiring similar levels of skill and responsibility should offer similar compensation (comparable worth). Others believe women will be better off if they choose careers in higher-paying fields (i.e., jobs now most often held by men).

3. Women workers with four or more years of college had an average income only slightly above men who had

(a) one to three years of high school.[3] You might assume that an elementary school teacher is paid more than a garbage collector, but this is not necessarily true. People who believe pay scales should be determined by the amount of education, skill and responsibility needed to perform a job point to this statistic as evidence that changes must be made. But until then, you must be selective about the career you prepare for.

4 and 5. In 1981, women constituted:

(c) 6.3% of the skilled craft and kindred workers and

(d) 2% of all carpenters.[4] This statistic is used by those who argue that women are simply not going into the higher paid job categories. In fact, though, there have been barriers for women and minorities trying to enter the skilled trades in the past. Some of these barriers still exist, but improvement can be seen. While it may not take any more training to become a skilled craft worker than it does to become a hairdresser, the craftsperson makes much more money. Do you think more women should become carpenters and skilled workers? Or do you believe hairdressers should be paid as much as workers in the trades? Both arguments have merit and are worth thinking about.

6. Of the fastest-growing *private* companies in America,

(d) 4% are run by women.[5] More women than men are now starting their own businesses, so this figure should change. Women entrepreneurs usually state that they went into business for themselves because there were not enough opportunities for advancement in their previous jobs. They also seem to feel that, in their own companies, their earnings will be more in line with the effort they put into the job.

7. The average net worth of a man running one of the "INC. 500" companies is $4.8 million while the average net worth of a woman running an "INC. 500" company is:

(a) $1.6 million.[6] There are many possible reasons. Perhaps the women spend less time at their jobs than their male counterparts due to family responsibilities. Maybe men are able to get more financial backing for their enterprises. Or they might be willing to take more risks than women. The businesses they are involved in will also play a role in potential earnings. Since women, in general, haven't been running their companies as long, it may just be a matter of time before they build their businesses to the size of some of those run by men. Anyway you look at it, though, a net worth of $1.6 million isn't bad.

8. (c) 10% of working women earn more than $20,000 per year.[7]

Compared to this figure, the $1.6 million we talked about above seems miraculous. But miracles have nothing to do with it. In general, women who earn high salaries have a skill and a plan. They have confidence in their ability to succeed, and that confidence allows them to take some calculated risks. They don't assume that any field is closed to them. Lower-paid women, on the other hand, continue to hold traditional "women's jobs." Since it is difficult to support a family on less than $20,000 a year, young women are well advised to follow the example of the higher-salaried females.

9. (b) 7% of employed women in the United States work in managerial positions.[8]

The woman manager with her three-piece suit and briefcase has become the symbol of the working woman, but in fact this description fits only a small percentage of female employees. When you think about working, move beyond this stereotype. It is just as valid to imagine yourself in the robes of a judge, the uniform of an airline pilot or the overalls of a mechanic.

10. In 1984, one out of every (d) 4 women earned less than $10,000 per year when working fulltime.[9]

Most of these women are part of the "pink collar ghetto," employed in low-paying jobs held almost exclusively by women. If they must support themselves (and nearly half of all employed women do), their lives are difficult. If they must support families, their lives are nearly impossible.

11. In 1960, women in managerial positions earned 58% of the male wage; in 1980 they earned (c) 55%.[10] Of course, there were fewer women managers in 1960. Since women are just beginning to enter management positions in larger numbers, some of the wage discrepancy exists because women managers are likely to be younger and have less experience. Still, women have made greater progress in entering previously male-dominated careers than they have in receiving equal pay or comparable promotions.

Childhood Choices

The choices of childhood can have an effect on decisions we make later in life. Some of those choices were imposed on us by parents, teachers, or circumstance. Some we made ourselves. Think back to your early years to answer the following questions. Check the box that most closely reflects your choices.

AGES 3–6

1. If you were taken to a toy store when you were three to six years old, were you more likely to choose as a gift:
   - ☐ a. a doll, stuffed animal or imitation makeup?
   - ☐ b. a truck, building blocks or a rubber ball?

2. What would your parents have been more likely to give you for Christmas when you were six years old:
   - ☐ a. a doll, stuffed animal or imitation makeup?
   - ☐ b. a truck, building blocks or a rubber ball?

3. What is the first occupation you remember telling a someone you wanted to pursue?

   _____
   fill in
   - ☐ a. This is a career area in which there are more women than men.
   - ☐ b. This is a career area in which there are more men than women.

AGES 8–12

4. When you were eight to twelve years old, how much TV did you watch per day?
   - ☐ a. 2 hours or more
   - ☐ b. 1 hour or less

5. At the same age, how were you likely to spend your time at recess?
   - ☐ a. playing hopscotch, jump rope, four square or talking to friends
   - ☐ b. playing softball or baseball, football, volleyball or basketball

6. After school, were you more likely to:
   - ☐ a. play indoors, watch TV or visit a friend's home?
   - ☐ b. play outdoors, explore, shop or visit a recreational facility?

AGES 10–14

7. When you were ten to fourteen years old, which set of chores were you most likely to do at home:
   - ☐ a. dishwashing, babysitting, cleaning, making lunch?
   - ☐ b. doing yard work, washing the car, taking out trash?

8. If you were to run for a student government office, would you have been more likely to run for the office of:
   - ☐ a. vice president or secretary?
   - ☐ b. president or treasurer?

9. When you were twelve, which of the following statements would you be most likely to heed:
   - ☐ a. Best friend: "Don't take the advanced math class. It meets at the same time as chorus. You don't need math, anyway."
   - ☐ b. Parent or teacher: "Chorus is nice, but I think it would be a serious mistake not to take the advanced math for which you're qualified."

10. Were you more likely to earn money:
    - ☐ a. babysitting?
    - ☐ b. having a paper route?

11. Did your mother work outside the home?
    - ☐ a. no
    - ☐ b. yes

12. If she did, was she employed in a position:
    - ☐ a. held by more women than men?
    - ☐ b. held by more men than women?

Answers follow.

111

Interpretations

If you answered "a" to a majority of the questions, you grew up with "traditionally feminine" values. On the plus side, that means that you are likely to be good at socializing, collaborating, and maintaining relationships. But you had little opportunity to develop your physical skills, or to practice competing and taking risks. You might not have thought about all the alternatives open to you at this point in your life. Or you might not have the confidence to go after what you really want. Let's examine your responses more closely.

1 and 2 The "a" toys reinforced preparation for family roles, while the "b" toys reinforced workforce and career preparation. While it is important to be good at relationships if you want to succeed in work, it is also important to take action and master skills in the areas in which you may need some practice.

3 Studies show that as early as age three and four, children's perceptions of, and aspirations to, adult work are sex-role stereotyped. Young women who answered "a" and young men who answered "b" probably already were beginning to think of some jobs as the only appropriate careers for their sex.

4 If you watched any significant amount of television when you were young, you were undoubtedly bombarded with stereotyped messages concerning sex roles in our society.

5 Jump rope. hopscotch, four square and other turn-taking games place little emphasis on competition, while games like softball, volleyball, basketball and football encourage competitiveness, risk taking and team building. These three qualities are important skills for success in the working world.

6 Answer "a" suggests that you tended to choose a secure, low risk environment rather than one offering exploration and freedom.

7 Housekeeping and child care typify girls' chores at home, while boys are more likely to perform outdoor tasks.

8 Secretary and vice president are supportive roles to the more active parts played by the president and treasurer. Leadership and decision-making skills are important in many higher-paying careers.

9 Your peers usually have a more traditional attitude about future options. Adults tend to be more flexible about sex roles and more realistic about the importance of planning for your future.

10 Babysitting teaches family skills, while having a paper route is more career-oriented.

11 and 12 Role models are very important when you begin to think about your future, and mothers are *very* important models. If you had a mother who worked, you will be more open to a career. If your mother worked in a non-traditional field, you are less likely to put artificial limits on your hopes and dreams.

As you read the rest of this book, keep reminding yourself that the options presented here do apply to you. Believe in yourself! Attitudes and expectations can be changed. You can do it! Start thinking positively and stride confidently into your future!

If you answered "b" to most of the questions, you have probably already made some choices that will help you be successful in your future career. You are more likely to be open to a wide variety of career choices, and you will probably enjoy the exploration process which will lead you to a good decision. You are at least somewhat comfortable taking risks and competing with others. The strategies presented in this book should not present any major problems for you.

Conduct a Personal Survey

What do the women and girls in your life tell you about appropriate work for a woman? Below, write the names of 20 females you know well. In the second column, indicate either the job they currently hold, or the career they are preparing for. In column three, write an **F** if that job is held by more women than men, an **M** if it is held by more men than women and an **E** if the sex distribution is about equal in that job.

Name	Career	M, F or E
1.		
2.		
3.		
4.		
5.		
6.		
7.		
8.		
9.		
10.		
11.		
12.		
13.		
14.		
15.		
16.		
17.		
18.		
19.		
20.		

Now evaluate your survey results and come up with some conclusions of your own. Write a news release regarding the results of your poll below.

Results of Major Poll on Women and Work Announced

The results of a major poll conducted by _____ and announced today indicate important trends in the work patterns of women. Namely: _____

_____
_____
_____
_____
_____
_____

If these trends continue, Ms./Mr. _____ feels there will be significant repercussions throughout society. The good news is that _____

_____
_____
_____
_____

But problems exist, as well. Ms./Mr. _____ believes that these might include _____

_____
_____
_____
_____

After analyzing the situation carefully, Ms./Mr. _____ has the following advice for young women about to embark on a career: _____

_____
_____
_____
_____

The Truth About "Non-traditional" Careers

Sometime in the past few years, a well-intentioned person coined the term "non-traditional" describing jobs that are usually held by men. Young women who are encouraged to enter these fields are showing some resistance, and maybe that is to be expected. After all, most young women are not interested in being "non-traditional." On the contrary, like most people—maybe more than most people—young women want to be like everybody else. This is an understandable position. But it will cost you.

There is a great deal of *tradition* behind the kinds of jobs most women hold:

> They are traditionally low in pay.
>
> They are traditionally low in status.
>
> And they are traditionally low in the amount of control they allow you to have over your life.

Men's jobs are traditional, too—traditionally higher-paying.

Maybe it's time we set aside the "traditional" and "non-traditional" labels and give all jobs more accurate descriptions. Let's just call them lower-paying/lower control (instead of traditional) and higher-paying/higher control (instead of non-traditional) careers.

Higher Pay, No College Necessary

Turn back to Question 3 on the answer page to the Wage Gap Quiz on page 109 of this chapter. When we talk about men with less education making more money than women with college degrees, we are usually talking about men with a marketable trade or skill. In general, there is a lot more money to be made in the work world of "blue collars" than in the "pink collar ghetto." These jobs even have higher incomes than careers in teaching and social work—fields that require four years of college, and are dominated by women.

You can see this as a problem—or as an opportunity. You don't necessarily have to spend four years in college to have a higher-paying job. A year or two in vocational school can prepare you for any number of careers that offer compensation *at least* equal to that of many college-educated professionals. Most of these jobs can be flexible as well.

Vocational Education— The Best-kept Secret

Let's make some comparisons. On the following page, construct a bar graph to indicate the average annual salary for each career listed. How do the salaries relate? Use a colored pencil to color in the bars of the careers requiring four years of college. Using a different colored pencil, color in the bars of those careers that require vocational school or on-the-job training. Now evaluate which jobs would also allow for some flexibility in scheduling of hours to be worked. In pen, make diagonal slashes to set those careers off. (See auto mechanic as an example.)

	Average Annual Salary	Years of College	Years of Vocational School
Elementary teacher	$20,500	5 yrs.	
Librarian	$23,200	4+ yrs.	
Newspaper reporter	$20,000	4 yrs.	
Nurse, (B.S.)	$24,000	4 yrs.	
Social worker	$19,400	4 yrs.	
Auto mechanic	$27,000		2 yrs.
Welder	$19,240		2 yrs.
Meatcutter	$26,000		2 yrs.
Electrician	$35,600		2+ yrs.
Plumber	$32,800		2+ yrs.

> High wage occupations mean opportunities for women to learn vocational skills to pay bills.
> —Charlotte C. Gore

[Bar chart showing wages for occupations: Elementary teacher, Librarian, Newspaper reporter, Nurse (B.S.), Social worker, Auto mechanic (~$27,000), Welder, Meatcutter, Electrician, Plumber]

There are other advantages to a vocational education. Tuition is usually very low in comparison to that at a college. With financial aid, it could even be free. Even if you can't afford to go to college, you can probably put yourself through vocational school. Schools are located in most population centers, so probably you could live at home, if money is a problem, or commute to school if for some other reason you cannot relocate. Vocational schools are making an effort to promote equity between the sexes. They offer dozens of different programs. Sound good to you? Why not call or write the school nearest you for more information, or talk to your school counselor or career advisor.

Some Jobs to Consider— Some Jobs to Forget About

Just knowing whether a job is usually held by a man or a woman is not enough information when making career decisions. As society changes—and it changes quickly—some jobs become obsolete, while others come into demand. The need for people in other fields varies with the economy or the population. For example, there are expected to be few openings for college or university faculty in the next ten years because the number of college-age students has decreased. There are more *younger* students coming up, though, so the demand will *increase* later on. A few years ago, there was an over supply of engineers. Now they are in great demand. But, according to the Bureau of Labor Statistics, the **fewest** number of job openings in the next decade will be in these jobs:

Postal clerks
College and university faculty
Compositors and typesetters
Stenographers
Butchers and meatcutters
Mail carriers
Communications equipment mechanics

Air traffic controllers
Drafters
Farm equipment mechanics
Health and regulatory inspectors
Plasterers
Boilermakers
Telephone operators

If the career of your dreams is on that list, you might consider going into one of the following job areas instead. Job satisfaction is of the utmost importance, however. The career to plan for is one that you love *and* one that will let you earn a living. For your consideration, the Bureau of Labor Statistics lists these jobs as the **fastest-growing** in the next ten years:

Computer service technicians	Occupational therapists
Legal assistants	Health services administrators
Computer systems analysts	Physical therapists
Tool programmers, numerical control	Mechanical engineers
Computer programmers	Podiatrists
Electrical engineers	Nuclear engineers
Electrical and electronics technicians	Registered nurses

If you are leaning toward a career not on either list, the prospects of finding a job in that field are probably average. But you need to do some research to find out what the job openings are likely to be. Your services may not be in as great demand as those of professionals on the second list, but if you love what you do, you will undoubtedly do it so well that your chances of success will be good.

Also keep in mind that in this quickly changing world it is probable that you will have between two and five careers before you retire. With the right attitude and the right skills, adapting to career changes can be exciting and rewarding. Flexibility is the key.

Patterns for Happiness

Women with higher salaries and job flexibility seem to have many things in common.

1. They have made a commitment to get the **education or training** they need to establish themselves in their field.
2. They are willing to **delay childbirth** until parenting can be the enjoyable experience it should be, not just another source of stress for an already overworked woman.
3. These women have **set up support networks** for themselves, whether they consist of family, friends or spouse. They are likely to have a husband who shares the household responsibilities, a housekeeper or cleaning person, as well as professional child care.
4. And they have ways to **"get away from it all;"** whether through hobbies, vacations or their own retreat place.

Women like these seem to have found the formula for happiness. They have:

Something to do.
Someone to love.
Something to look forward to.

The same formula applies to men. In the past, men were supposed to concentrate their energies on making a living. They often were away from home too much to take an active part in parenting. Their marriages sometimes didn't work out well, either. An epidemic of stress, divorce and heart disease has changed the lives of many American males. They are finding that the pleasures of family life are not to be missed. As more women share the responsibility of providing an income for the household, some of the pressure has been taken off men. They are beginning to see that they, too, need the balance that comes from a fulfilling job, friends and family, and time to do the things they care about.

Happy and successful men and women also share some important skills and attitudes. You will learn more about these in the following chapter.

REFLECTIONS

Chapter Seven
Skills & Attitudes That Will Give You Control

> I'm a great believer in luck, and I find the harder I work the more I have of it.
> —Thomas Jefferson

> One is not born a genius, one becomes a genius.
> —Simone de Beauvoir

Skills and Attitudes

If you are ever asked to choose just two things to bring with you into the future, consider these: the right skills and the right attitudes.

As society and technology evolve, necessary skills will change. But a sound education will help you adapt with a minimum of discomfort. The right attitudes, on the other hand, haven't changed for years, and show no signs of doing so.

In this chapter, we will examine these basic requirements for career success.

The Five Cs of Control

In the years since the original Sleeping Beauty took her famous nap, there has been a career rehabilitation movement among Good Fairies. Now, instead of bestowing their young clients with beauty, ball gowns and ingenious modes of transportation, Good Fairies are giving them something more important: control over their lives. Nice as a kiss and a ride on a white horse may be, they are decidedly fleeting pleasures. They don't hold up well alongside the satisfaction that comes from being in charge of your own life, of having what we call the Five Cs of Control: Competence, Commitment, Confidence, Creativity and Courage.

When you don't have control of your life, you are susceptible to problems as diverse as stress and boredom, having more obligations in your life than you can handle, or losing the things you value most. Unless you feel that you are in control, you cannot even enjoy your successes. With the 5 Cs on your side, however, you will know how you reached your present life situation, where you're going next and how you're going to get there.

Competence

Maria's Story

All Maria's friends teased her about her passion for learning. She would read everything from *The Wall Street Journal* to philosophy texts to volumes of modern poetry. She studied maps, cookbooks and computer manuals with equal intensity. If there was any piece of information Maria didn't know, she knew where to find it. Maria considered everything in her life—school, her job, relationships, hobbies—as an opportunity to gain knowledge. She used her education to develop skills—as many skills as she could. She wanted to be able to *do* things, and to do them *right*. Maria found that knowledge, education and competence were of value in every area of her life. Her competence was an important factor in the control she felt she had over everything she did.

In his book, *Megatrends*, author John Naisbitt says, "The new source of power is not money in the hands of a few, but information in the hands of many." Since it is generally easier to gain information than money, the coming of the information society is a great benefit for most people. Naisbitt goes on to say, ". . . Knowledge is not subject to the law of conservation: It can be created, it can be destroyed, and most importantly it is synergetic—that is, the whole is usually greater than the sum of the parts."[1]

In other words, adding to your knowledge in one field will often lead you to see new relationships or make new discoveries in other areas, as well. Your knowledge and your competence are things you can continue to develop throughout your life. No one can take them away from you. Develop them, use them and treasure them. Learning *about* things and learning *to do* things are lifelong tasks. There are many ways to keep on learning when you are out of school. Consider professional organizations, extension classes, seminars, professional publications, lectures and, of course, books.

In which areas do you feel most competent now? Are you good at math or chemistry? Can you program a computer or fix a flat tire? Give yourself credit for all these things. Then think about areas in which you would like to improve your competence. There are probably skills that would be useful to you, or things that would just be fun to know. List three of them here and describe your plan.

___

Maria knew she needed to become familiar with computers. So she started to learn word processing. Below is Maria's plan for gaining competence in this vital skill.

New Skill Learning Word Processing on Computer

Maria's Plan Research available learning opportunities in my community.

Sign up for and complete a class series.

Volunteer to do word processing at local charity to get practice.

New Skill ___

Your Plan ___

New Skill ___

Your Plan ___

New Skill ___

Your Plan ___

Commitment

Belinda's Story

Belinda wanted to be a lawyer, but fulfilling her dream wasn't easy. When she was a sophomore in college, her father died and she had to move back home to help her mother. There wasn't enough money for her education anyway, her mother pointed out. Belinda started working nights until she made enough money to return to college on her own. Exhausted from working and studying, she didn't do well enough on her law school entrance exams to get into the school she wanted to attend. She was better prepared when she took the test again six months later. During her second year of law school, she broke her leg in three places and was immobile for six weeks. Instead of falling behind in her classes, she had the sessions taped and hired a tutor to help her keep up with her classmates. When she graduated with honors, she took a job with a firm known for its unwillingness to promote women to partnership status. Belinda did her job so well she became the first woman partner.

Ricardo's Story

Ricardo's commitment took a different path. As a member of the city council, he became concerned about the city government's pattern of employment. Few women or minorities were employed in management positions. And men seemed to be paid more than women, whatever their jobs. Ricardo was convinced that something had to be done. He talked to the mayor, who told him it was hopeless—with the financial problems the city faced, there was no way to rectify the inequalities. Ricardo thought differently. He began to confer with union leaders, civil rights groups and women's organizations. They supported his efforts, and agreed to stand behind him. He brought the matter before the city council. At first, the council refused to discuss the matter. When Ricardo persisted, they agreed to talk about it. And they voted against his proposal—five times. Some of his supporters wanted to give up, but Ricardo stood firm. He organized a demonstration, started a letter-writing campaign and took out full-page ads in the newspaper, urging those in favor of his plan to speak up. They did. The council couldn't ignore the problem any longer, and a program to provide equal pay and equal opportunity was approved.

While just about everyone has a dream of some kind, only a few have the kind of persistence Belinda and Ricardo had. Their commitment gave them a sense of purpose. They believed in something enough to follow it through. And, because they persisted, they finally succeeded. Success like Belinda's not only adds to your self-esteem, but makes others seek you out when they need a job done well. Success like Ricardo's adds to the well-being of us all.

There are detours and potholes in everyone's life. But, if you are determined to meet your goals, you won't let obstacles stop you (however much they may slow you down). Many people stop short of their goals because they hadn't counted on any kind of hardship or delay. But life is difficult for everyone. If you realize this, you won't be permanently discouraged by the often small—and too often enormous—roadblocks we all encounter.

List three or four major commitments you have right now:

1. _____
2. _____
3. _____
4. _____

What are some possible detours? _____
_____

What will be the biggest commitments you will make in the next 10 years? _____
_____

Assume you want to be a medical doctor. What commitments will you need to make?
_____
_____

What commitments will you need to make if you want to be happily married? _____
_____

> Always bear in mind that your own resolution to succeed is more important than any other one thing.
> —Abraham Lincoln

Confidence

Contrary to what TV commercials tell us, we can't really buy confidence along with an underarm deodorant, dandruff shampoo or any other product. When we are young our family can help build our confidence (just as you can help pass it on to your own children). When we get older, it can only come from within.

Confidence may be one of the most important gifts you can give yourself. If you have it, you will be better at making decisions and taking chances. You will be able to deal with both failure and success—in your career and in your personal life. If you are not already a confident person, you need to take steps to become one. It's not easy, but it isn't impossible either. To begin to build up your confidence:

Make a list of all the things you do well. Are you good at sketching? At athletics? Can you use a camera or a computer? Are you a good friend? Can you play the piano or ride a skateboard? Make your list as complete as you can.

Give yourself credit for those accomplishments. Many people concentrate on what they do poorly rather than what they do well. Don't be one of them. Learn to accept compliments, while you're at it. Believe them!

Reward yourself when you succeed at something. If you earn a good grade in geometry this semester, for example, you might buy yourself a new sweater or an album you've been wanting. Before you accomplish a task, the thought of the reward might motivate you to do your best. Afterwards, the reward serves as a reminder of what you can do.

If you are not confident in certain situations, act as though you are, anyway. Pretend you are confident, à la Jimminy Cricket. You will probably fool other people and you may even convince yourself. For example, you might not feel confident when you apply for a job. But if you dress the part, look confident and tell the interviewer what a terrific job you will do for the company, you are more likely to get the job. Getting the job will help you feel more confident, so it will be easier for you to act that way in the future.

Remember nobody can make you
feel inferior without your consent.
—Eleanor Roosevelt

AFFIRMATIONS

Use affirmations. Affirmations are short, positive statements that you repeat to yourself over and over again. Eventually, your subconscious begins to accept these statements as truth. You then begin to act as though they are true. And they become true! There are such things as self-fulfilling prophecies, after all. For example, if you tell yourself repeatedly that you are a good speaker before you give a presentation, you are likely to do a better job. If you tell yourself that you are an outgoing person, it will become easier to start a conversation with someone you don't know at a party.

It may sound like glorified "wishful thinking," but it's much more than that. Affirmations have been shown to be effective in reprogramming the way you think—especially the way you think about yourself. To work best, they need to be repeated often, at a time when you are relaxed and receptive to the messages you give yourself. Say your affirmations aloud and then, as you go through your day, act *as if* the messages are true. Some other hints for using affirmations successfully include:

1. Use your own name in the affirmation. "I, _____, am a confident person."

2. Use the present tense in your affirmations, as in the example above. Pretend that the statement is *already* true.

3. State your affirmations as positively as you can. Say "I, Sue, am a confident person" rather than "I, Sue, am not going to be shy anymore." Doing it this way helps create a positive mental image.

4. Make your statements brief and clear. Be sure they feel right for you and believe in them!

Belinda might have used the following affirmation:

Situation	Affirmation
Getting into law school	I, Belinda, am going to be a lawyer.

In what areas do you need to develop more confidence? Can you think of some affirmations for those situations? Make your list below.

Situation	Affirmation
_____	_____
_____	_____
_____	_____
_____	_____

> I pretended to be somebody I wanted to be, and I finally became that person.
>
> —Cary Grant

Creativity

Sarah's Story

Sarah was determined to go to college, even though she couldn't afford it. Because she lived in a small town, some of the common ways to earn money were not available to her: There was no fast food restaurant, no boutique, not even the possibility of a paper route. Sarah, however, was determined—and creative. One day she made a list of possible ways to earn her tuition. She thought of:

    Getting an academic scholarship.

    Getting an athletic scholarship.

    Taking out a loan.

    Having a series of fund-raising parties—with the funds going to her college account.

    Raffling a color TV to be bought with the $400 she'd saved from babysitting.

    Writing to ask someone famous to be her sponsor.

    Entering contests.

    Studying the stock market and investing her $400.

    Writing a novel about the life of a small town girl who really wants to go to college but can't afford to.

    Training her dog, Zippy, for a career in show business.

    Taking night classes at college while working during the day.

Sarah's final list was much longer. Some of the ideas could be eliminated immediately (Zippy never did have much charisma). Others, she thought, just might work. And one of them did. Sarah now has an MBA (Master's in Business Administration) and is a rising star with an enterprising and creative public relations firm.

A creative person like Sarah, knows that there is more than one way to solve a problem. Creativity is especially important in a time of great change, such as ours. There aren't enough role models for young women who plan to have both a career and a family, and society offers little help. Perhaps that is an advantage. You won't be saddled with a lot of "right answers" to your problems. But you will need to use your own creative abilities in order to make your life work.

And you do have creative abilities. Everyone does. You solve dozens of problems every day: getting dressed, making dinner, finding a way to get a date with someone you like. All solutions need a touch of creativity. Use yours as often and as consciously as you can. Instead of relying on the same routines and the same answers in your daily life, try to think of something better—or at least something different. Is there a faster way to make a bed? A more enjoyable way to earn money? A better way to research a science project? Another use for the three mis-matched mittens in your drawer?

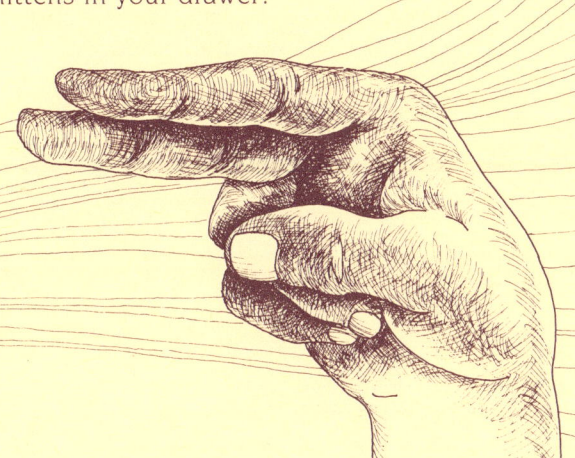

Follow these steps to come up with some new ideas:

1. Define the problem. Do you need more money? More time? A better grade in math? Be as clear and as specific as possible.

2. Get as much information as you can concerning the problem.

3. Like Sarah, make a list with as many possible solutions as you can think of. Don't censor yourself. Write down every solution that comes to mind, no matter how ridiculous it seems.

4. Take a walk. Play a game. Go to bed. Stop thinking about the problem for awhile, and let your subconscious evaluate your ideas.

5. Come back later and decide which idea is best.

1. What is a problem you would like to solve in a creative way?
   Problem:_____

2. What information do you need concerning this problem?
   _____
   _____

3. What are the possible solutions?
   _____
   _____
   _____
   _____
   _____

4. Let your subconscious take over for awhile. Then come back and look at your list of solutions again. Which seems best to you?
   _____
   _____
   _____
   _____
   _____
   _____
   _____

5. What is your plan for putting it into effect?
   _____
   _____
   _____
   _____
   _____

Courage

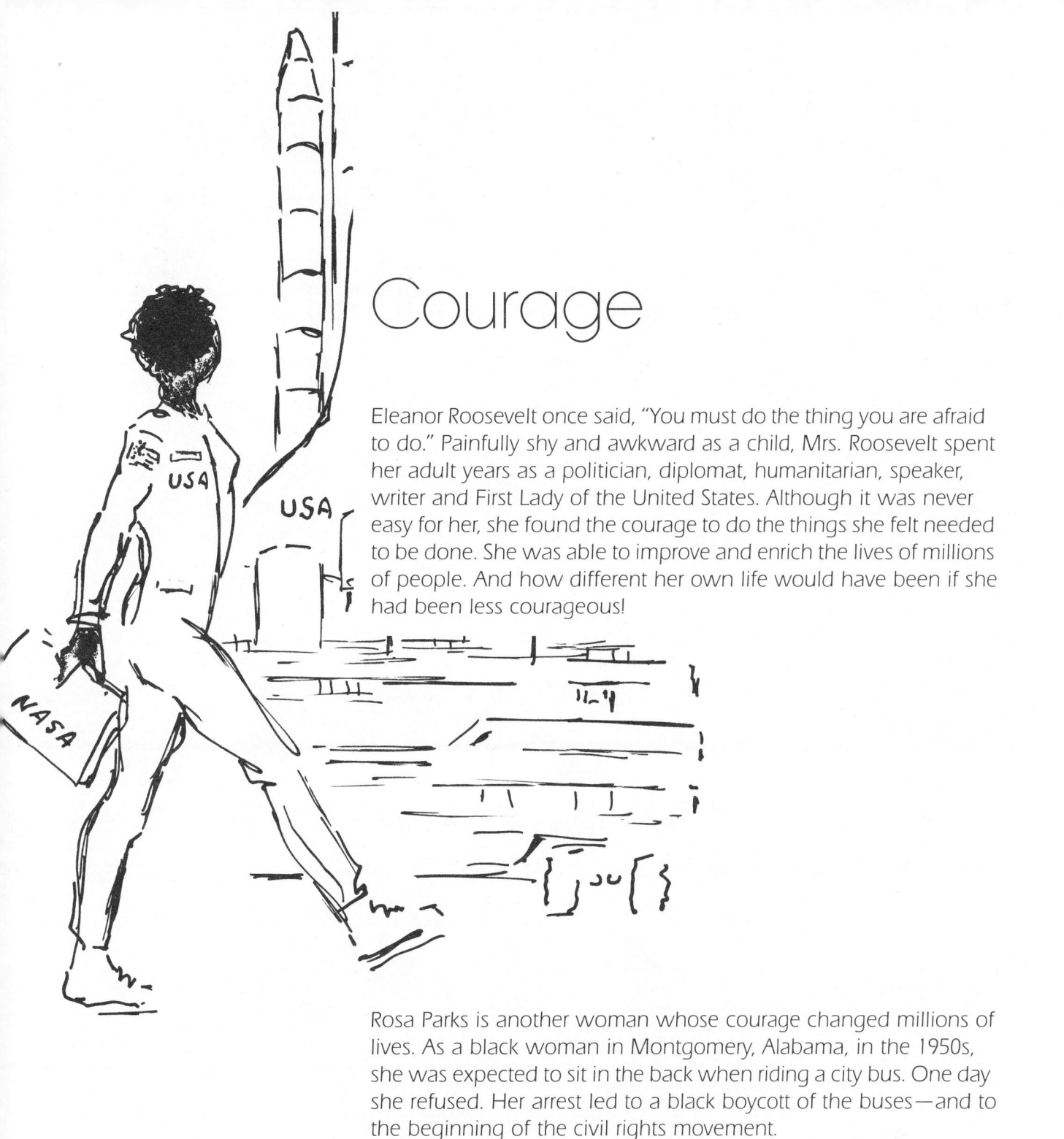

Eleanor Roosevelt once said, "You must do the thing you are afraid to do." Painfully shy and awkward as a child, Mrs. Roosevelt spent her adult years as a politician, diplomat, humanitarian, speaker, writer and First Lady of the United States. Although it was never easy for her, she found the courage to do the things she felt needed to be done. She was able to improve and enrich the lives of millions of people. And how different her own life would have been if she had been less courageous!

Rosa Parks is another woman whose courage changed millions of lives. As a black woman in Montgomery, Alabama, in the 1950s, she was expected to sit in the back when riding a city bus. One day she refused. Her arrest led to a black boycott of the buses—and to the beginning of the civil rights movement.

Courage is the ability to evaluate a situation, consult your feelings about it and then take whatever action you deem necessary. Sometimes it's frightening, and sometimes it involves risk, but, if you can take this kind of calculated risk, your life will be infinitely more rewarding.

When you stop to think about it, nearly everything you do involves some kind of risk. Riding your bike to school is risky. But then, so is driving a car or riding in a bus. Walking can be dangerous. And staying home is the most risky of all. (What kind of future will you have without an education? And, besides, nine out of ten accidents happen in the home!)

You are taking risks when you choose a career or a marriage partner, and when you attempt to balance your job and your family life. Of course, it is also risky not to prepare for a career, or to try to raise a family on an inadequate salary. So there's really no getting around it.

Still, some people are better at taking risks than others. They are more decisive and assertive. They have the ability to maintain their values under pressure. And they have a few ways to help decide whether a risk is worth taking. They might take the bottom line approach: "What is the worst that could happen? Is that so bad?" They might reframe the question: "What could happen if I don't take this risk?" They might think of ways to help reduce the odds of failing, or they may combine all three strategies.

How good are you at taking calculated risks? Could you honestly make the following statements about yourself? Circle your response.

I am not afraid of competition.	Yes	No	Undecided
I am an assertive person.	Yes	No	Undecided
I am capable of making difficult decisions.	Yes	No	Undecided
I stand up for the things I believe in.	Yes	No	Undecided
I will volunteer for a difficult assignment if success would be rewarding for me.	Yes	No	Undecided
I am willing to take on added responsibility in exchange for added knowledge, experience or recognition.	Yes	No	Undecided
Sometimes I try things just to see if I can do them.	Yes	No	Undecided
I would never let the fear of failure keep me from trying something I really wanted to do.	Yes	No	Undecided
I don't become discouraged if my first attempt at something is not a total success.	Yes	No	Undecided
I think Woody Allen was right when he said, "If you're not failing now and again, it's a sign you're playing it safe."	Yes	No	Undecided

Are you "playing it safe"? List something you would like to do but have not attempted out of fear.
_____
_____

What is the worst thing that could happen if you don't succeed?
_____
_____

What is the worst thing that could happen if you don't try?
_____
_____

What is the best thing that could happen?
_____
_____

Is it worth the attempt?
_____
_____

How can you increase the odds of success and reduce the odds of failure?
_____
_____

> Only those who dare to fail greatly can ever achieve greatly.
> —Robert F. Kennedy

The Importance of Math

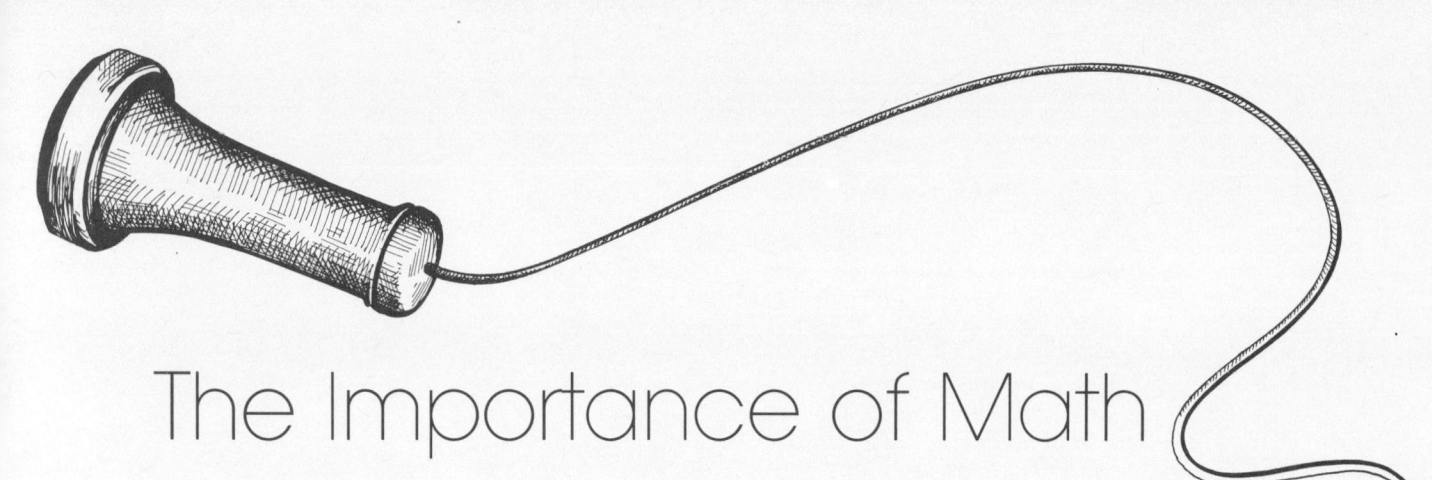

Kim's Story

Kim was the math whiz of the fourth grade. Fractions, decimals, long division—they were all simple to her. But by the time she reached junior high, things had changed. Kim found herself getting Cs in math instead of the A's she was used to. She avoided her homework and looked forward to the day when she could put math behind her and start taking interesting classes like "The History of Synthetic Fabrics" or "Topics in Silk Flower Arrangement."

When Kim registered for her classes at school, she filled her schedule with subjects she found different and interesting. Several days later, she received a call from her guidance counselor. He asked if Kim had given much thought to her future career. "I don't know," Kim replied. "I guess I'd like to do something exciting that pays a lot of money." "Do you suppose that the salary of your average flower arranger ranks in the top ten, Kim? Your past grades show that you're an intelligent young woman. You could be anything you want to be. But you're sabotaging your future if you don't take advanced math classes now. Without them, you won't even be eligible to get into most of the college programs that lead to high-paying careers. I want you to reconsider your schedule for next year."

Kim thought about it. She wondered what had become of the math ability she had shown as a child. It couldn't just evaporate. "Math is just like any other skill," she told herself. "I can do it and I won't cheat myself out of a rewarding future by continuing to act as though I can't. Even if I have to work harder or get special help to catch up, I will take math—and I will succeed."

Kim's story is a familiar one. Although girls generally do well in grade school math, they seem to lose interest in it in junior high. By the time young women enter high school, they are likely to give up the subject entirely. This is unfortunate because many of the most desirable careers require a solid math background. It is also a tragedy because so many young women really believe that they are incapable of doing well in math. This is simply not true. *Recent studies show that there is virtually no difference in math ability between the sexes.* The difference in performance is due to attitude toward math, perception of how it might be valuable and influence of parents, teachers, and other important individuals in a person's life.

Let's examine some of these factors more closely.

Attitude = Success

At any age, your success in math is influenced by attitudes—your own and those of your relatives, peers and teachers. As a youngster, you probably received support and encouragement for doing well in math from your parents and teachers. Maybe their enthusiasm spurred you on to even greater accomplishments. As you grew older, though, attitudes may have changed. Perhaps you started to think that success in math would make you unpopular. Maybe you didn't think math would have much application in your future career. Parents and teachers may have begun to encourage boys more than girls because they subconsciously believed the myth that girls are less gifted in math. Your story might be totally different.

Use the graph below to find out. With a ballpoint pen, mark your own attitude toward math at each grade level and connect the dots. Do the same to indicate your parents' attitude toward your math education, this time using a pencil. Now use a felt pen to show your teachers' attitudes toward your math education.

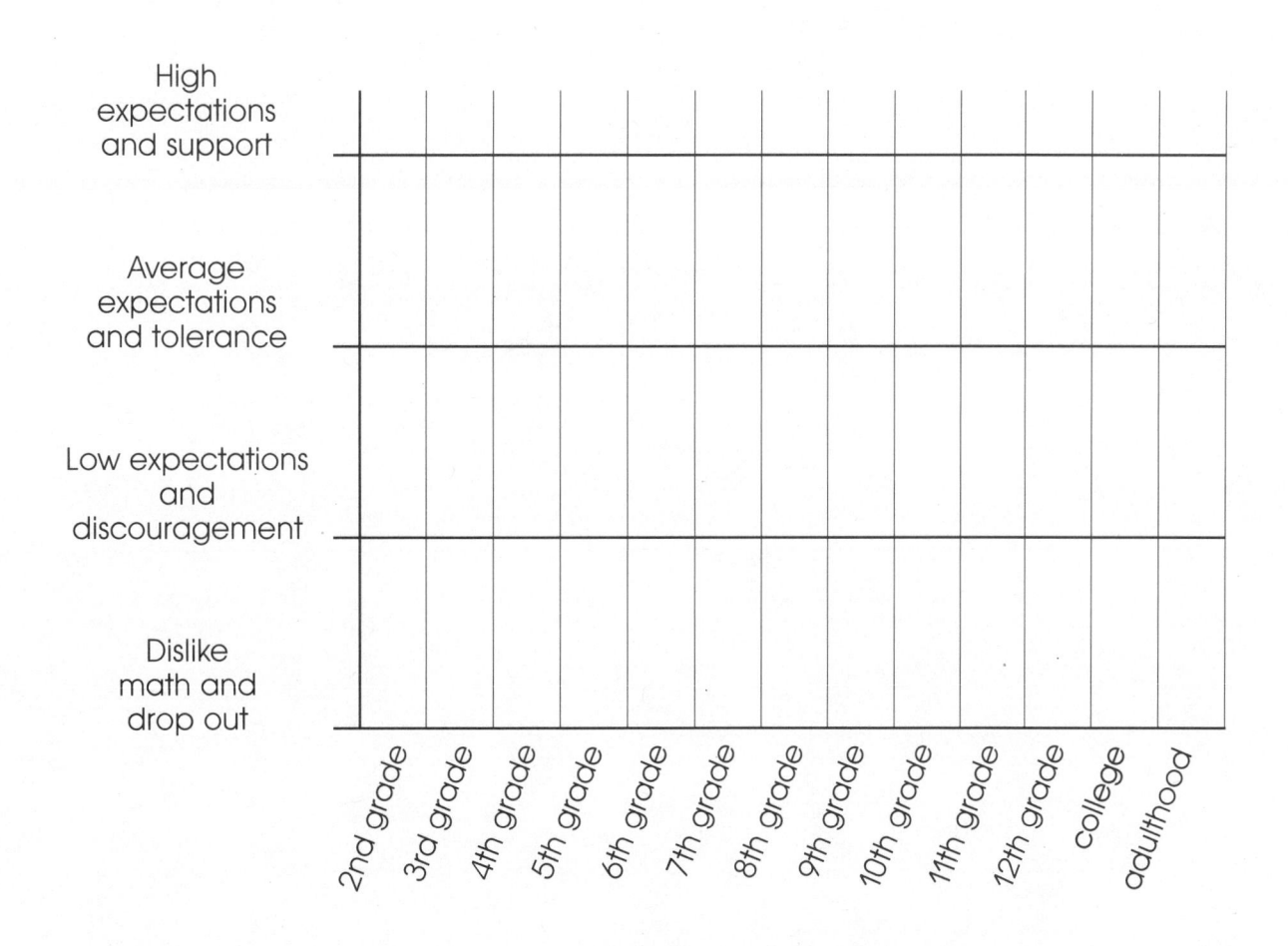

What patterns do you see on your graph? Do the attitudes you have recorded bear any relation to your math classes and grades at each level?

Getting in Shape for Math Success

If you've ever been involved in a sport, you know that attitude and training are equally important elements of success. The team practices all week to become proficient in the physical aspects of the game. But an emotional coach, a crew of energetic cheerleaders and a stadium full of screaming fans help to provide that all important "winning spirit."

The same elements are needed for success in math. Be your own cheerleader and your biggest fan. At the same time, don't forget that help is available if you need it. Form or join a math support group, find a tutor or sympathetic teacher or take special remedial classes if you need to.

Earlier in this chapter we talked about affirmations and how they can help you succeed by improving your attitude. This is a good place to put affirmations to work. Repeat the following statements to yourself daily, or whenever you find negative feelings about your math abilities creeping into your conscious mind.

I, _____ (your name), enjoy math.

I, _____ (your name), do well at math.

With enough training and time, I, _____ (your name), can figure out any problem.

I, _____ (your name), know math and rational thinking are important to my future success and happiness.

I, _____ (your name), am a problem solver.

What are some other affirmations you might use?

_____
_____
_____
_____

They are able who think they are able.
—Virgil

Math—The Critical Filter

Maybe you aren't aware of it, but an overwhelming majority of high-paying careers require a solid math background. Math has been called "The Critical Filter" because only those who complete upper division math classes in high school are eligible for many of the career programs in college or vocational school. Math serves as a kind of sieve: Only those who succeed in it pass through to the highest-paying and most flexible careers.

The careers listed below are the same we dealt with in Chapter 4. Those that we've written a "No" beside require no upper division math. If we have indicated "Yes/HS" beside a career, it calls for three to four years of high school math (two years of algebra, one of geometry). Those careers we've noted as "Yes/College" require college level math or science in addition to the high school math.

Social worker	Yes/HS
File clerk	No
Chiropractor	Yes/College
Physical therapist	Yes/College
Switchboard operator	No
Secretary	No
Nurse (vocational)	Yes/HS
Bank teller	No
Architect	Yes/College
House painter	No
Flight attendant	No
Librarian	Yes/HS
Optometrist	Yes/College
Photographer	No
Receptionist	No
Shop clerk	No
Elementary teacher	Yes/HS
Dentist	Yes/College
Psychologist	Yes/College
Electrician	Yes/HS

Turn back to the graph on page 75 in Chapter 4. Do you see a correlation between math and salary level?

_____

Take another look at the graph on page 75. What is the relationship between math preparation and job flexibility?

_____

Do you think the time spent on your math studies now will pay off in increased time with your children later?

          Yes   No

A Word Problem

With a solid math background, you will have more options for a career offering both higher salary and flexibility—the keys to successfully combining career and family life. Also, math will give you an attitude toward solving problems that is highly valued by employers and highly transferable to any endeavor you care to undertake. Still, some people shy away from math. Maybe they think it involves too much work or it is too risky.

Why do you think some people are unwilling to take math classes? _____
_____
_____

Has anyone ever told you not to worry about math because you won't need it?   Yes   No

Do you think algebra or geometry requires more studying than other classes you might take?
Yes   No

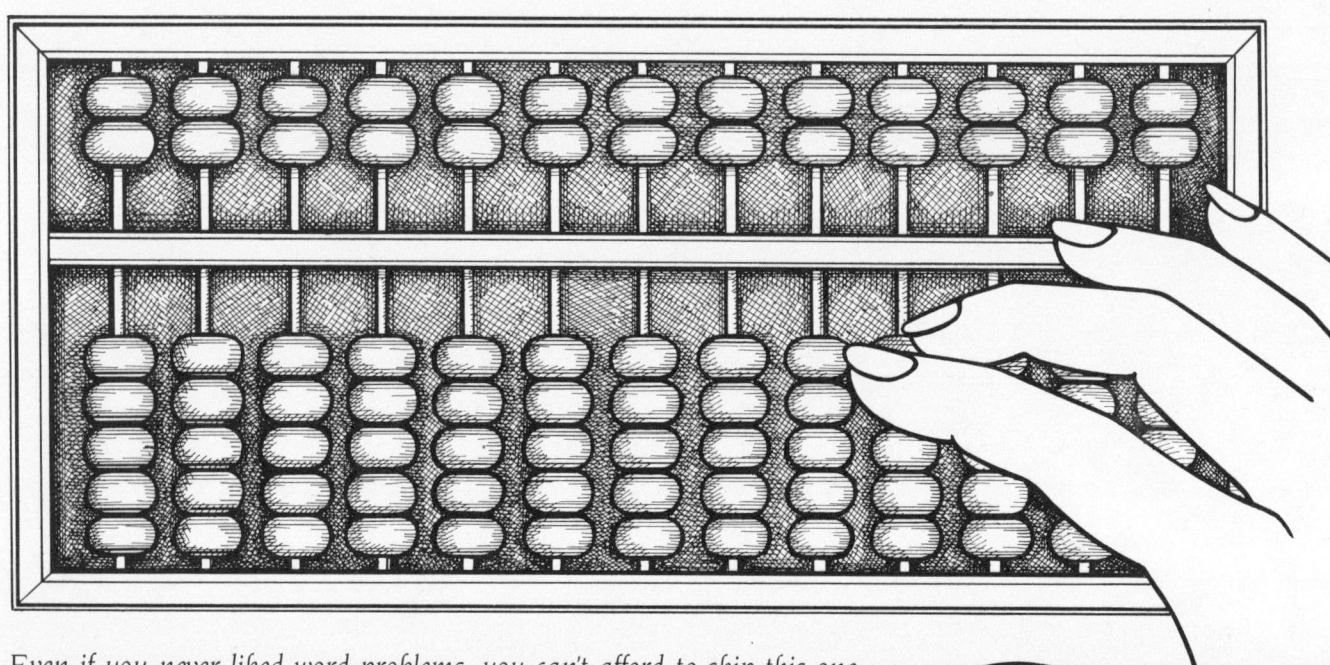

Even if you never liked word problems, you can't afford to skip this one... it could be the most important math problem you will ever solve.

144

WORD PROBLEM

How many hours per week would you need to spend on your math homework?

_____ (a)

If math required an average of _____ (a) hours of study each week, (use the figure you entered in (a) above), how many hours of study would be required to complete four years of math? Each school year is 36 weeks.

4 years × 36 weeks × _____ (a) number of hours studying math per week

= _____ (b) total number of hours spent studying math in high school

According to the United States Department of Labor, the average teenage woman can expect to spend 27 years in the workforce while the average teenage man can expect to spend 39 years. How many years do you think you will spend in the workforce between the ages of 18 and 65?

_____ (c)

If a full-time job takes 2,080 hours per year (40 hours per week × 52 weeks per year), how many hours could you spend in your career over a lifetime?

_____ (c) years in the workforce × 2,080 work hours per year

= _____ (d) hours in career over your lifetime.

What is the ratio between the hours spent studying math in high school and the total number of hours spent in your career?

_____ (d) ÷ _____ (b) = _____ (e)

Therefore, for every hour you spend studying math in high school, you will spend how many hours in the workforce?

_____ (e)

Look at the figures above once more. Is the time invested now worth the future dividend of a higher salary and flexible career?   Yes   No

Still not convinced? Let's take this problem solving one step further.

Choose a career from the list on page 143 that *does not require math* and that you have some interest in. Then turn to page 74 and find the average hourly rate of pay and enter below. Divide the annual salary by 2080 to find the hourly rate.

CAREER TITLE _____ = $ _____ **(s)** average hourly rate of pay

Now choose a career *requiring either high school or college math* from the same list on page 143. It, too, should hold some appeal for you. Again turn to page 74 and find the average hourly salary.

CAREER TITLE _____ = $ _____ **(r)** average hourly rate of pay

To determine how much **each hour of studying in high school is worth in dollars of future earnings**, first determine the difference in hourly wages of the two careers above.

$ _____ **(r)** − $ _____ **(s)** = _____ **(t)**

Next, multiply that difference by the total number of hours you can expect to hold a job (figure **d** from the previous page). This will give you the difference in lifetime earnings between the job that requires a strong math background and one that does not.

_____ **(d)** × $ _____ **(t)** = $ _____ **(w)**

One more way to look at this is to divide the difference in lifetime earnings **(w)** by the number of hours spent studying math **(b)** to get the increased future earnings for every hour spent studying math in high school.

$ _____ **(w)** ÷ _____ **(b)** = $ _____ of increased future earnings for every hour spent studying math in high school.

Think about that the next time you sit down to study your math!!!

Time invested now + math education = Higher pay + flexibility = Increased options for parenting time.

Sissy and Sally's Story

Sissy and Sally had not seen each other for years when they met one day while shopping. After half an hour of lively talk about "the good old days," conversation turned to the present. Sally had a prosperous dental practice, and was quite pleased with her life. Sissy was less satisfied. "I never thought I'd be supporting a family," she said. "But here I am with two kids to provide for, and the best job I could find is as a receptionist making $5.00 an hour."

Sally remembered how, back in high school, Sissy had teased her about her insistence on taking math classes. Sissy didn't think it was necessary to work that hard. Now, ironically, Sissy was working harder than Sally *ever* did—for very little reward of any kind.

Sally gave Sissy a reassuring hug and suggested that she go back to school for further training. "You don't automatically lose your ability to learn math at age 22," she said. "With a few courses in night school, you could be on your way to a better paying, more satisfying job."

As Sally drove home that afternoon, she added up the figures in her head: she was now making $30 an hour, or $25 more than her friend. Sally had studied math for five hours a week in high school so, if she is in the workforce for 27 years, she will have studied one hour for each 78 hours she works.

The difference in lifetime earnings between her job and Sissy's ($1,404,000) divided by the number of hours she spent studying math (720) equals Sally's hourly earnings for studying high school math.

In other words, over her lifetime, Sally will earn $1,950 for *every hour* she spent studying math in school!

In short, a strong math background is essential.

- It gives you more options in choosing a satisfactory career.
- It gives you the right attitude toward problem solving, an attitude that will be helpful in every job and every area of your life.
- It gives you more control over the direction of your life.
- It can greatly enhance your earnings.
- It may increase your parenting time, and adds to the earning power and flexibility in your career.

It's never too late to get the math background you need. If you are already out of school, consider going back. It will almost certainly help you get a career that allows more options for parenting.

> You may be disappointed if you fail,
> but you are doomed if you don't try.
> —Beverly Sills

Putting Your Skills To Use

There is nothing like practice to build your skills and attitudes. If your math background is not what it might be, use the following exercise to formulate your plan for improvement. If you are already working toward a strong math background, the exercise will give you practice using your 5 Cs.

State your goal or the problem to be solved.

To acquire a good math background that will qualify me for a career which will support a family.

Attitude: Is this problem or goal important to you? Why?

Do you believe that a strong math background is needed for success in most of the careers compatible with parenting? Yes No

Competence:

How do you plan to go about acquiring math competency? List the actions you plan to take below, in the order you plan to take them.

_____
_____
_____
_____
_____

Commitment:

What kind of commitment will your math studies require? Describe below.

_____
_____
_____

Confidence:

Now, see yourself as capable of accomplishing your goal. Write three to five affirmations you could use to help you achieve your math goals.

_____
_____
_____
_____
_____

Creativity:

    Explore creative ways of achieving your goal and detouring roadblocks. List below all the ways you can reach your math goals.

_____

_____

    Can you foresee any problems or roadblocks you might encounter on the road to math competency? If so, describe them below.

_____

_____

    Use your creativity to make a list of **all** the solutions you might use to overcome those problems.

_____

_____

    What solutions seem best or most workable to you? Circle two of them.

Courage:

    What risks must you take? Are the risks worth the possible rewards? What is the worst thing that could happen to you if you try to improve your math background, but don't succeed?

_____

_____

    What is the worst thing that could happen to you if you don't even try to learn math?

_____

_____

    What is the best thing that could happen if you try?

_____

_____

    Does the possible success make it worth while to risk failure?   Yes   No

The planning and evaluation model you just used can be applied to any difficult problem you encounter while making your strategic plan or, for that matter, at any time in your life. You might use it to help you decide whether to attend college or vocational school, how you are going to do it, whether to become a free-lancer or set up your own business, or whether and when to have a child.

Your Own Planning Model

Now use the same model to reach another goal or solve another problem in your life.

State your goal or the problem to be solved. _____
_____

Attitude: Is this problem or goal important to you? Why? _____
_____

Competence:

    How will you become competent in this area? How do you plan to go about attaining your goal or solving your problem? List the actions you plan to take below, in the order you plan to take them.

    _____
    _____
    _____
    _____
    _____

Commitment:

    What kind of commitment must you make?

    _____
    _____

Confidence:

    Now see yourself as capable of accomplishing your goal. Write three to five affirmations you could use to help you achieve your goal or solve your problem.

    _____
    _____
    _____
    _____
    _____

Creativity:

Explore creative ways of achieving your goal and detouring roadblocks. List below all the ways you can reach your goal.

_____
_____
_____

Can you foresee any problems or roadblocks you might encounter on the road to your goal? If so, describe them below.

_____
_____
_____

Use your creativity to make a list of **all** the solutions you might use to overcome those problems.

_____
_____
_____

What solutions seem best or most workable to you? Circle two of them.

Courage:

What risks must you take? Are the risks worth the possible rewards? What is the worst thing that could happen to you if you try to reach your goal, but don't succeed?

_____
_____
_____

What is the worst thing that could happen to you if you don't even try?

_____
_____

What is the best thing that could happen if you try?

_____
_____

Does the possible success make it worthwhile to risk failure?   Yes   No

Communication Skills—
They Count Too

Fifty years ago, most American businesses produced industrial and consumer goods such as steel, coal and automobiles. Then businesses dealing with information and services started to grow, and increasing numbers of workers became involved in such fields as marketing, advertising, child care and counseling. We are now becoming known as "the information society." Our most important product is *what we know*!

But just having information is not enough. It is essential to be able to share that information with others. You must be able to communicate what you know, both orally and in writing.

Many students excel in one area, like science, language, social sciences or communications. There often seems to be a barrier between the different fields, however. Only a few students are accomplished in more than one. There is no known reason for the situation—the barrier exists only in the mind. If you can dismiss it and become one of the small number of people who are equipped with technical knowledge *and* the ability to pass it on in speech or on paper, or if you can analyze a situation *and* run a meeting, your services will be in great demand.

Invest In Yourself

Lola's Story

When Lola was 18, she inherited $20,000 from her grandmother. There were no restrictions—Lola could do anything she wanted with the money. She thought about buying a fancy car. She checked out the prices on a round-the-world trip. She talked with lawyers and stockbrokers about investing the money in real estate or mutual funds. Then she decided to invest the money—in herself. Lola used the money to put herself through college. She knew that her own knowledge was a kind of wealth that could never be diminished or taken away; that her education would pay a dividend no other investment could hope to match.

Education—not just math education, not just English, but education in general—is something to be valued and pursued. The more you have, the richer your life will be, in every sense of the word. Education means not only more earnings (though the lifetime earnings of a woman with a college education are likely to be 2½ times greater than the lifetime earnings of a woman who does not complete high school), but greater flexibility, more time and less stress.

As we've said before, education is a life-long process. It's never too late to go back to school, and it's *always* too soon to stop learning.

Education can increase your confidence and self-esteem, give you more control and add immeasurably to your enjoyment of life. Get all you can. You will never regret it.

> Native ability without education is like a tree without fruit.
> —Aristippies (435-356 B.C.)

153

REFLECTIONS

Chapter Eight

Keeping Your Life in Balance

You must learn to be still in the midst of activity and to be vibrantly alive in repose.
—Indira Gandhi

If you cannot find happiness along the way, you will not find it at the end of the road.

Balancing Your Life

Elise's Story

When Elise missed a meeting with her advertising agency's biggest client because she had, once again, run out of gas on the freeway, she knew she had to change something in her life—or her boss would change it for her. Elise's job security at that point was approximately equal to that of a 5'3" center for the Los Angeles Lakers. if she had not been the most talented art director in the business, she would have been out of a job. Elise just seemed to have problems organizing her life. Sometimes it was the job that suffered; other times it was her health or her family. Just last month, she completely forgot about her son's sixth birthday party when she became engrossed in a work project that didn't have to be completed for weeks. To make up for that mistake, she took both children to the beach for the entire weekend. When she got home Sunday night, she had to clean the house, do four loads of laundry, run out to the grocery store, pay the overdue bills, manicure her nails and try to make amends with her husband, who was complaining that she didn't seem to have much time for their relationship anymore. By the time Elise got to work on Monday, she was exhausted, sick to her stomach and so moody no one dared speak to her.

Elise's life is dangerously out of balance. Her life is so full that she has trouble knowing what to do first, what to do next and what not to do at all. Elise needs to set priorities for her career life, her family life and herself. And then she needs to make sure that she takes the time to meet her top priorities in each category.

Everyone needs balance in his or her life. For a woman with a family and a career, balancing is the only way to assure life satisfaction. Besides career responsibilities, even though things are changing somewhat, women still usually have major responsibility for child care, maintaining the relationship with their husbands and taking care of the home. Women also need to take care of themselves—if they don't have their health and their sanity, they won't be of much use to anyone.

On top of all this, or maybe because of all this, many women are saddled with guilt. They feel guilty for a) leaving their children, b) neglecting their husbands, c) loving their jobs, d) harboring waxy yellow buildup on their kitchen floors, e) not dealing with ring around the collar and f) not feeling guilty enough about a, b, c, d and e.

If your life is in balance, there is no reason for you to feel guilty about any of the above. A balanced life is one in which you give appropriate weight to your career, your relationships and yourself. No one can give precisely the same amount of time to each category every day of the year. You might occasionally set aside two weeks to complete a project at work. Maybe you will take a summer off to spend with your family or friends. Or you might need to get away by yourself from time to time. But, overall, you do need to devote time and planning to each segment of your life.

> When we speak about **career,** we are referring to the main activity in your life. While the most obvious career is paid employment, going to school can be a career, and so can taking care of a home. Your career might be managing your investments or working as a volunteer for your favorite political candidate or community charity. Over the full course of your life, you might have several *different* careers.
>
> **Relationships** refer to your activities with all the important people in your life: your spouse, children, relatives, parents, friends and co-workers. Work done for the benefit of others is also a part of this category. For example, time spent coaching a Little League team would count as time devoted to relationships.
>
> The last category is **self.** Since time spent sleeping can be charged to this category, you might be tempted to short-change yourself here. Some people need more time to themselves than others, but we all need to devote time to our health, our mental and spiritual development and the solo activities we find enriching. Count the time you need to meditate, worship in your own way or just think about things. Time to eat right, exercise and pursue your hobbies should be charged to this category, too.

The circle graph below demonstrates the distribution of an ideally balanced life.

Let's look at the balance in some other people's lives. In each of the circles below, draw lines to indicate what you think the graph of the person described would look like. What percentage of this person's time would be devoted to work? Self? Relationships?

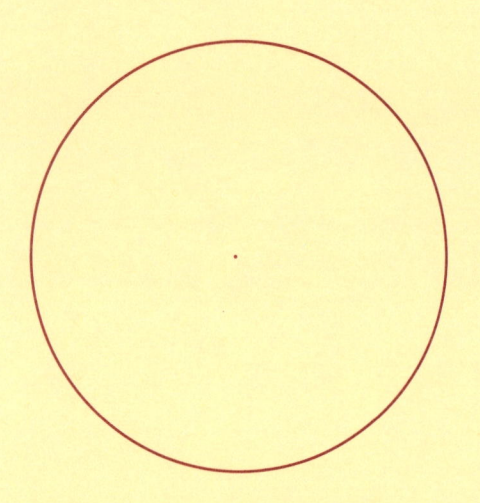

Joyce is a workaholic with a demanding family. Lately her health has begun to suffer.

Sally loves her job as a computer programmer. She's joined a health club and usually stops by for an aerobics class after work. Then she has her tennis lesson, and she practices her piano for an hour every day. By the time she's done all this, her daughter is usually asleep, so they communicate very little.

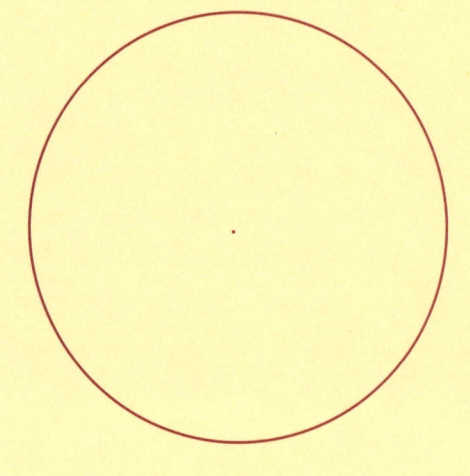

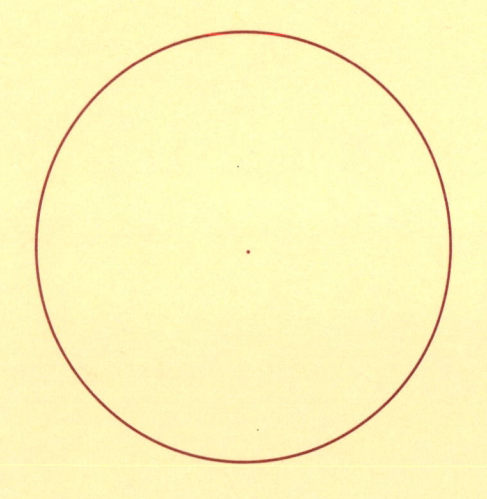

As a single parent, Chris feels doubly responsible to the children. They require so much time that keeping a part-time job in the pet store rather than taking a more demanding and more rewarding position that would also alleviate some of the money worries seems the only answer.

In this circle, draw a balanced lifestyle and *think* of a story to go along with it. Write your story below.

_____
_____
_____
_____

Complete a chart for a female friend or relative whose life may be out of balance. Write her story in the space provided.

_____
_____
_____
_____
_____

How balanced is your life? Make a chart for yourself and describe your situation. Are there things you need to change? If so, how do you plan to do that?

_____
_____
_____
_____

Getting Control

Vicki's Story

Vicki was troubled with a chronic inability—the inability to say "no." She felt that, if she was going to have a career, she had to give it everything she had. As a wife, she "had to" fill all those traditional roles, as well. And she certainly didn't intend to let her children suffer just because they had a working mother. The same rules applied to community service, housework, dealing with her parents and her friends. No wonder Vicki was always tired, irritable and likely to break into tears. By trying to be everything to everyone, she was under enough stress to bring down the Golden Gate Bridge.

Until recently, when people spoke of stress, they usually associated it with middle-aged male executives who went around barking at people and popping antacid tablets all day long. Today, the working woman, and particularly the working mother, is the most likely candidate for stress-related problems. The new stress stereotype is a woman who tries to do too much and thus leaves herself vulnerable to the effects of physical fatigue and mental exhaustion.

Interestingly, recent studies indicate that stress is linked to another characteristic—control. If you feel that you have control of your life, and the direction it is taking, you are less likely to find your lifestyle stressful, however eventful it may be. Turn back to page 127 and review the five Cs of control. Keep them in your life even when the demands of career and parenting make it difficult.

Some other ways to reduce the amount of stress in your life include:

Set priorities and don't expect to be everything to everyone.

Share or delegate responsibility when you can.

Use relaxation techniques and physical exercise to relieve stress.

Learn to be assertive. Say "no" to tasks not on your priority list.

Renegotiate your agreements with others if you cannot realistically do what you said you would, or if they are not following through on their commitments to you.

Get help from friends, family members or professionals if you need it.

Get organized. Make the most effective use of your time.

Give yourself credit for the things you do well instead of criticizing yourself for the areas in which you think you need improvement.

Your Health

Frank's Story

Because Frank was such a pleasant person, co-workers were constantly stopping at his desk to chat. Frank enjoyed brief conversations, but he found it hard to end them, even when he was getting behind in his work. As a result, Frank usually worked through his lunch hour, trying desperately to catch up. By the end of the day, he was hungry, tired and frustrated.

Dionne's Story

Dionne was the most competent secretary in her department. Whenever someone wanted a job done right, Dionne was asked to do it. She took pride in her reputation, and found it difficult to turn down assignments or ask for help, even when she was overwhelmed. As a result, she was usually the last one to leave the office. She was exhausted by the time she got home, but no one volunteered to help her fix dinner, and she couldn't bring herself to ask.

Nina's Story

With a full-time job and a five-year-old child, Nina never had a minute to spare. Still, when her son volunteered her services to sew costumes for his kindergarten class's spring pageant, Nina went along with the idea. The week before the pageant, Nina worked 'til 3 a.m. every night.

Good health is the basis of a balanced lifestyle. But when things get hectic, busy people tend to cut back first on the time they have allotted for themselves (which is usually not much to begin with). Is it really self-indulgent to take the time you need to sleep, eat correctly, exercise and brush your teeth? Remember that time spent taking care of your own physical and emotional health is beneficial not only to you, but to your family and career. As a healthy and well-rested person, you are in a better position to take care of others, to make decisions and to perform at your best.

Albert Einstein proved that energy cannot be produced or destroyed. But the lives of many people show that it can be dribbled away if basic needs are not provided for. How well do you take care of yourself? Indicate how the following statements apply to you by marking the appropriate column.

	Always	Often	Sometimes	Never
I eat three balanced meals a day.				
I get 7 or 8 hours of sleep each night.				
I exercise at least 3 or 4 times a week.				
I take at least one hour a day to do something I really enjoy.				
I have positive thoughts about my life and my ability to control it.				
I plan for a break or vacation every year.				

Setting Priorities

Making a plan is one thing. Making it work is quite another. You can easily lose sight of your lifetime goals as you try to navigate through a sea of tasks, errands and the crises of daily life. Like Elise, whose story you read at the beginning of this chapter, many people find it hard to establish even short-term priorities. The happiest and most successful people, however, never lose sight of either their short-term priorities or those things that have enduring meaning in their lives.

Short-term priorities need to be set daily or weekly. Each morning, you might ask yourself which two or three things you absolutely need to accomplish that day. It's a good idea to write them down, and cross them off your list when they are completed. Ask yourself, too, if these are things you need to do yourself. Can some of them be delegated to others?

Managing Your Time and Energy

Since it's impossible to do everything you think you should do in a given day, setting short-term priorities is a must. For this exercise, assume you are married and hold a job outside the home. You have two children. Try to visualize your life. Below is a list of tasks that might require your energy and time. But which are most important?

In column one, put a 1 beside those items that must be done; a 2 beside those you would like to do if there is time; a 3 beside those tasks you would undertake only if all your 1s and 2s were done; and a 4 next to those items you do not consider important enough to do.

	1	2	3
Go to work			
Buy groceries			
Polish silver			
Spend time with children			
Spend time with mate			
Vacuum			
Wash the car			
Read novels			
Watch TV			
Read newspapers			
Eat breakfast			
Exercise			
See friends			
Call your mother			
Give dinner parties			
Take classes in your career field			
Arrange flowers			
Bake cookies			
Grow your own vegetables			
Sleep			
Do laundry			
Make your own clothes			

	1	2	3
Take child to doctor			
Attend school play			
Clean cat box			
Pay bills			
Do volunteer work			
Ask for raise			
Paint the living room			
Take a vacation			
Cornrow hair			
Learn to play golf			
Join a professional organization			
Read professional journals			
Hire new secretary			
Return boss's phone call			
Get a sun tan			
Write letters			
Meet deadline for project at work			
Iron shirts			
Wash woodwork			
Take bubblebath			
Learn to use a computer			

Look at your list again. Is it necessary that you personally perform all the tasks you would like to see accomplished? What might your partner or children be able to do? Could you hire someone else to do some of these things?

In column 2, put a checkmark next to those tasks that could be delegated to someone else.

Finally, **in column 3,** put a C beside those items that are career-related, an R beside those that deal with relationships and an S next to self-related tasks. Look back at column one, and the items you assigned as number 1 priorities. Do you find at least one R task, one C and one S on this list?

Sometimes you "can't see the forest for the trees." Choosing between what you should be doing and what you would like to be doing can be overwhelming. Here is a simple method of setting priorities that might be helpful. This can be used for establishing either short-term or long-term priorities.

Let's focus first on setting short-term priorities. For this exercise use the time span of one week.

FIRST: In column one make a list of the activities and concerns that occupy your time in a week.

SECOND: Now add to that list any other activities you would like to include.

THIRD: In column two write how much time you spend or would like to spend on each activity.

Activity/Concern	Time

Now, in pencil, arrange the activities in order of importance. For example: *Sleeping 56 hours* should be right near the top. Change the time required for each activity if you need to.

There are 168 hours in a week, so your total in column 2 should not exceed that amount. You may have to eliminate some activities from your list. Continue arranging your activities until you are satisfied that you have a workable list.

Now go back and see if your activities or concerns fit into the career, relationship or self sphere of your life. In column 3 identify the sphere in which each activity fits. Are you making an attempt to balance your life?

Activity/Concern	Time	Career Relationship Self
	Total time	

Working through this exercise will help you focus on your priorities, preferences and desires and come up with a realistic list. It could be adapted to help you establish long-term priorities. Just change the time span to one year, two years or even five years.

Long-term priorities also need to be considered as you make your daily plans. You may tend to overlook them, since they are not always as clear or pressing as your short-term obligations. But they are often more important. For example, if your long-term priority is being admitted to the college of your choice, sending for admission requirements is essential early in your school career. Because it seems less urgent than, say, finishing an English paper, you may keep putting it off if it is not on your list.

If you are just beginning to make your life plans, you will want to review and re-set your long-term priorities often. Your attitudes and values may be changing rapidly at this stage. Or, as you gather information, you may decide that last week's priority holds little attraction for you now.

During different phases of your life, it is natural that you will have different priorities. If you have small children, for example, they will probably be your main concern. At certain times in your life, your top priority might be your job or your health. During these times, it may be necessary to temporarily short-change the other parts of your life. That is all right, as long you are making a conscious choice, one that you will re-evaluate often.

So You Want to be a Wonderwoman

While no one can be a Superwoman—or should even try to be—there are a few Wonderwomen (and Wondermen) who seem to excel in both their professional and personal lives. These people are not trying to live a myth, as would-be Superwomen do. They have made conscious choices to pursue the kind of life they are living. They are blessed with certain traits and abilities, but they still don't "have it all". Like the rest of us, they have had to make certain trade-offs. For example, most Wonderwomen have little time to themselves. It would be a mistake for someone who needs a great deal of private time to even attempt this lifestyle. But it can be exciting.

Susan's Story

Susan is a national organizer for environmental issues. She and her husband, Bob, an attorney, have two children. They provide room and board for a student who, in return, helps with housework and child care. Susan makes frequent business trips, and loves them. Jet lag is unknown to her, maybe because she's always been able to function with just five or six hours of sleep a night, anyway. When she is home, she and Bob spend early evenings with the children and then attend a social, political or professional function nearly every week. Susan enjoys her colleagues as much as her friends, and she feels so strongly about her work that she finds these dinners and events totally enjoyable. Her weekdays are tightly scheduled, but she prefers them that way. Susan gets easily bored if she isn't actively involved with someone or some task. Yet she plans for rest and family time as diligently as she plans her career activities. She and Bob take the kids on a long camping trip every summer, and spend most weekends at their family cabin in the country.

There aren't many people who can keep up a life like Susan's for long. Could you? Unless you can honestly answer "yes" to **all** of the following questions, you should probably not attempt it.

	Yes	No
Do you have exceptionally good health and stamina?	☐	☐
Can you happily get by with less personal time than most people require?	☐	☐
Do you like your work so much that you have a hard time distinguishing between business and pleasure?	☐	☐
Do you have the sense of commitment and the positive attitude needed to succeed?	☐	☐
Are you willing to prepare yourself with the necessary education?	☐	☐
Can you manage your time? Are you good at setting priorities and delegating responsibility?	☐	☐
Do you consistently schedule time for rest and vacations?	☐	☐
Do you have a good support system (family, friends, household help)?	☐	☐

Remember: We all make trade-offs. No one can "have it all". But, with careful planning, you can have the things that are most important to you. Don't worry about the rest.

REFLECTIONS

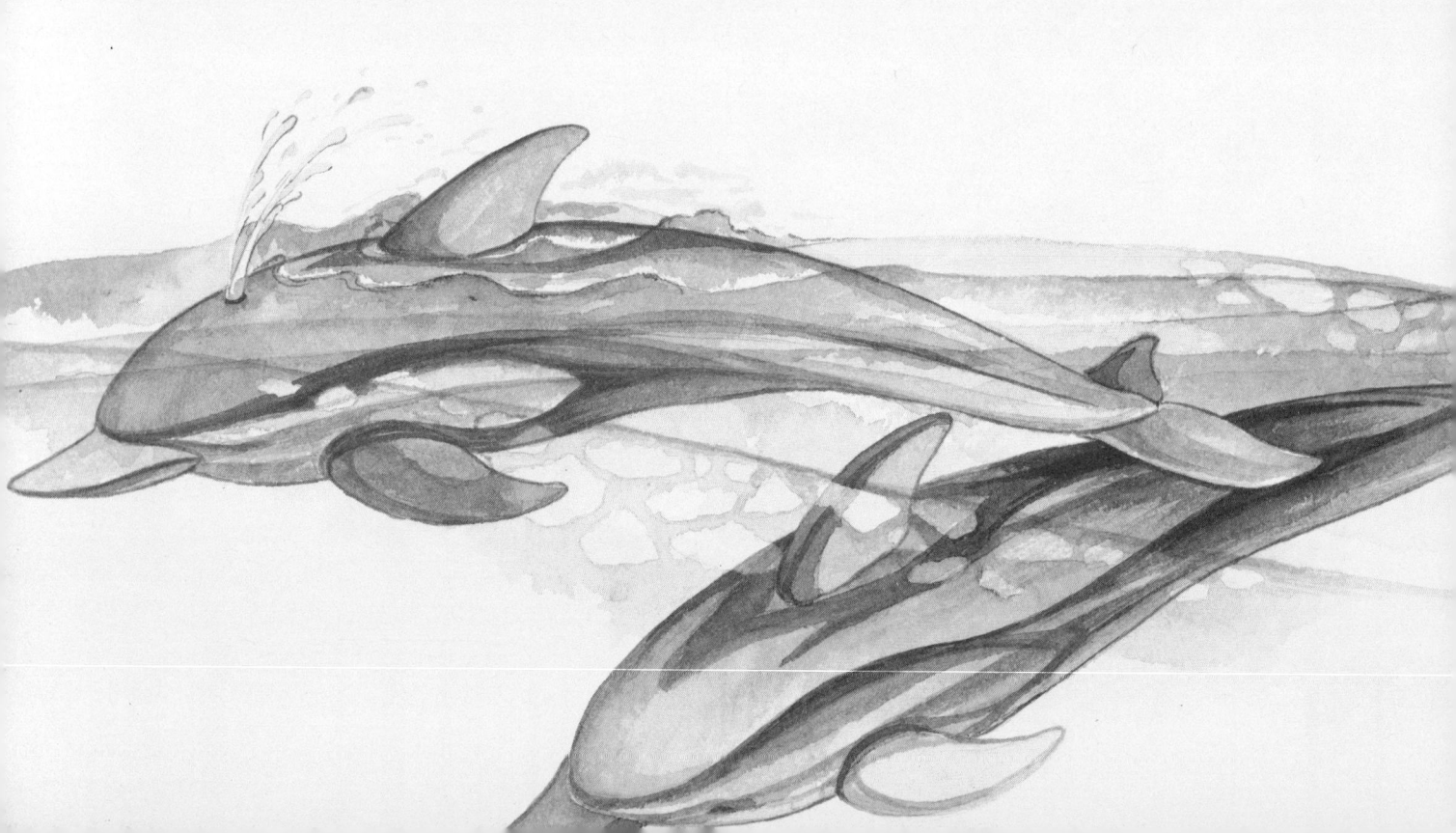

CHAPTER NINE

Managing Your Relationships

If thou wouldst marry wisely,
marry thy equal.
—Ovid

The basic discovery about any
people is the discovery of the
relationship between its men
and women.
—Pearl Buck

Relationships

A Modern-Day Fairy Tale

When Prince Andrew of Great Britain married Sarah Ferguson in July, 1986, romantics around the world breathed a collective sigh of relief. In this commercialized, computerized and complicated world, there is still room for true love, they said. And it came with all the trimmings: titles and castles, golden coaches and white horses, uniformed men with medals and swords, beautiful women in long beaded gowns and industrial-sized diamonds, cheering throngs of people, and the blessing of the Queen.

But this royal wedding was quite different even from the wedding of Andrew's brother, Charles, five years earlier. The press wanted to know *more* than how the couple met and when they first realized they were in love and what kind of engagement ring the bride would receive. Andrew and Sarah discussed where they would live and how the marriage would affect the groom's career and whether the bride would keep her job. Even fairy tales, it seems, aren't what they used to be.

The whole business of choosing a mate has become much more complicated. Thirty years ago, many people assumed that the husband would have a career, the wife would stay at home, they would have three children, a dog and a station wagon, and the family would move whenever the man's job required it. Today, a young couple needs to ask many more questions before making a commitment: What kind of relationship do they want to have? Will they both work? Will they both work full time? Do they want to have children? If so, what kind of child care do they want? Are both partners willing to share in parenting and housework? How will they decide what to do if one partner has a job offer in a different city?

Marriage can begin to sound more like a business arrangement than a love match. But, as Sarah's and Andrew's story shows, there is still room for romance. We can't tell you with whom to fall in love, so we'll settle for raising some questions and showing you some of your many, many options.

Trina and Ron's Story

Shortly after Trina was named assistant professor in the history department of a small college, she found she was pregnant. She was excited about having the child, but she didn't think she could take much time away from her new responsibilities on the job. Her husband, Ron, was a police officer, and was also attending night school to earn his master's degree in criminology. Ron and Trina agreed that she shouldn't endanger the new position she'd worked so hard to get. But they both thought their new baby should have a parent around during the day. So Ron left his job on the police force to care for the baby, and Trina took over parenting in the evening, leaving Ron free to go to class.

Allison and Warren's Story

Allison was a successful businesswoman who, at thirty-five, had not found a man she wanted to marry. She knew who she was looking for: someone a little taller, a little older, a little smarter, and a little more successful than she was. Those criteria narrowed the field considerably. Allison had a good friend, Warren, who was always proclaiming his love for her, but she didn't take him seriously. Warren owned a carpentry shop, liked camping trips and hadn't worn a tie since he graduated from high school. Still, he was the best friend of every woman, child and dog in his neighborhood. One day, after a particularly wonderful visit with Warren, Allison thought with a start: "Who says I need a powerful man in my life? It's nice to be loved by someone like Warren." She called and asked if he really meant all those proposals. He did.

Marjorie's Story

Marjorie grew up thinking that she would eventually marry and have children, but it hadn't turned out that way. As an international tour guide, she was on the go all the time. She had a wide circle of friends—male and female—and she loved her job. Sometimes she wondered what had become of that expectation she'd had for a more traditional lifestyle. But on reflection, she knew that she liked her life just the way it was and had no time for a husband or children of her own.

As these stories illustrate, the old-fashioned Ozzie and Harriet relationship is largely a thing of the past. It hasn't been replaced by any one new pattern, but by a kaleidoscope of possibilities. Today we talk about things like two-career households, househusbands, single parents, delayed motherhood and a rash of terms that would have been mentioned only as oddities just a few years ago.

Dual-Income Households

The dual-income household is one of the most common of these new terms. It refers, of course, to a home in which both partners have outside jobs. The arrangement poses problems about who will do the housework and who will take care of the children, but few people still suggest that this way of life will soon disappear. It simply isn't economically feasible for many families to live on one income anymore. And there are some real benefits for the entire family in dual-income families.

Liz and Larry's Story

Larry was a mid-level manager with a company that manufactured construction equipment. Liz was an air traffic controller. When Larry's company went out of business during the last recession, he lost his job. During the year it took him to find another position, the family lived on Liz's income alone. They had to cut back on spending, but at least they were able to keep their home, and no one went hungry.

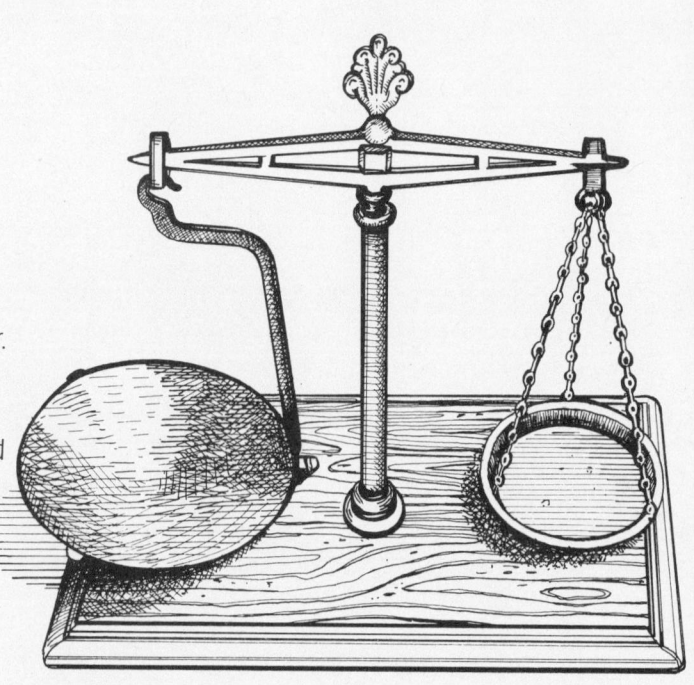

Debbie and Mike's Story

Debbie and Mike were partners in their architectural design firm. They believed their equality at work spilled over into their personal lives as well, and strengthened their relationship. The sizable income their two careers generated permitted Debbie and Mike to have many choices about the way they lived. They were pleased to be able to have the kind of child care so important to them both, and to hire someone to do most of the housework, leaving more time for family activities.

Celie and Gretchen's Story

Celie was a buyer for a department store, and Gretchen worked part-time as a sales representative for a toy company. Both were single parents. Celie's income was adequate to pay the mortgage, but she didn't have much money left for child care or help around the house. Gretchen's income varied from month to month, which made her life unpredictable. The two women teamed up, with Gretchen and her kids moving in with Celie's family. Gretchen's help with expenses left Celie with more disposable income, and Gretchen didn't have to worry about ending up in the street if she couldn't pay her rent one month.

OTHER REASONS FOR MAINTAINING A DUAL-INCOME HOUSEHOLD...

Marriage satisfaction for both partners seems to improve when they both earn enough to maintain their basic standard of living.

In today's real estate market, it is usually necessary for a family to have two incomes in order to purchase a home.

The income from two jobs allows the family a higher standard of living in all areas.

Two incomes can strengthen the relationship between father and children if the man takes on more parenting chores.

Family security goes up with the knowledge that, should one partner lose his or her job, there would still be an income for the household.

A higher household income makes it possible to have more choices about paid housework and child care.

With a working wife, a man is relieved of the burden of being sole support for his family. He has more freedom to take a lower-paying job that he would like better, to go back to school and retrain for a new career, or to work fewer hours, and he has more time for his family.

As more women enter the workforce, businesses are being forced to make some accommodations for parenting among their employees of *both* sexes. More companies already make provisions for maternity and paternity leaves; a few have on-site child care facilities.

Women now in decision-making positions within corporations, unions and political caucuses and committees are able to see that this trend continues.

ON THE OTHER HAND...

Good child care is expensive—and difficult to obtain. In 1983 the California Commission on the Status of Women determined that there were 1.2 million licensed daycare slots available in the country—and 23 million children who needed them.

Few American companies have made concessions to allow for good parenting. It seems they are still operating on the premise that all their employees are men with wives at home all day to take care of the children.

Housework still needs to be done, whether there is someone home full time to do it or not. It is still most often the woman who ends up doing most household chores. She, therefore, has two jobs.

Trying to balance career, family and housework leaves millions of women exhausted and over-stressed much of the time.

Which leads us to the next topic...

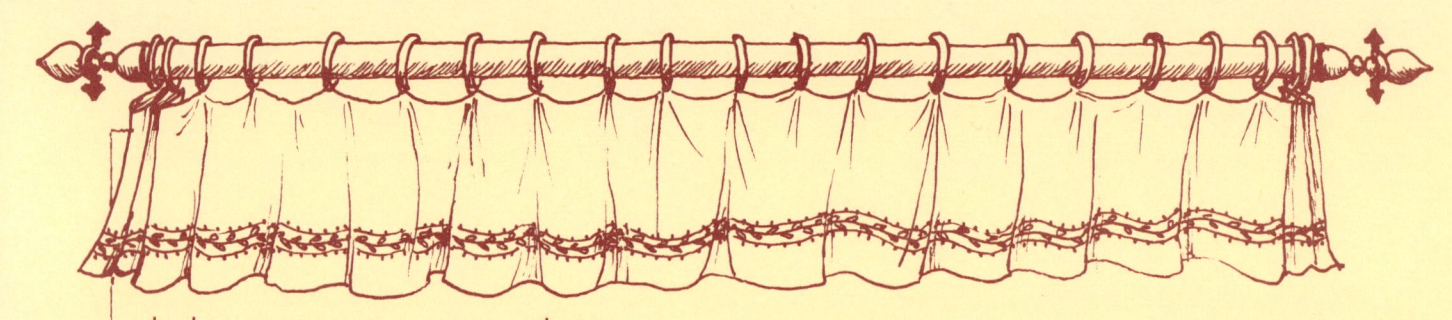

Housework:
See Yourself as Management...
Not Always as Labor.

As you discovered in the chapter on balancing your life, you can't do everything. This is particularly true when it comes to doing housework after a full day on the job. One way to deal with household tasks is to decide what's important to do. Then ask yourself if it is important *who* does it. Many chores can be delegated to other family members. Some of the most common tasks are listed in the following exercise.

In the **first column** beside each entry, list the kinds of skills needed to perform the chore.

In the **second column,** write down the age at which a person usually acquires those skills.

In the **third column,** note whether the task is limited to males or females, or if both sexes could be expected to do an adequate job.

For example:

TASK	SKILLS	AGE ACQUIRED	SEX
Vacuuming	Walking Turning switch Guiding machine	1+ 3 6–7	Either Either Either
Washing dishes			
Dusting			
Mowing lawn			
Taking out garbage			
Doing laundry			
Cooking			
Changing baby			
Washing windows			
Cleaning bathroom			
Folding clothes			
Buying groceries			
Putting groceries away			
Picking up after the family			
Watering plants			
Making beds			

Even with help from the family, you may find yourself overwhelmed by the chores of daily living. Some other options for getting things done without totally wearing yourself out are:

- having a cleaning service
- redefining your standards
- hiring a neighborhood teenager to run errands, mow the lawn, etc.
- having a lawn care service
- ordering groceries from a store that delivers
- using catalogs and ordering over the phone instead of shopping
- making use of shopping services offered by many department stores
- having potluck parties or trying shared entertaining instead of doing all the work yourself
- cutting back your hours at work to have adequate time to do housework yourself
- living in a condominium or a smaller home that requires less maintenance
- having a college student live with you in exchange for help around the house
- deciding not to have children

Can you think of other options?

_____
_____
_____
_____
_____
_____
_____

There are many alternatives. The worst one is trying to do everything yourself.

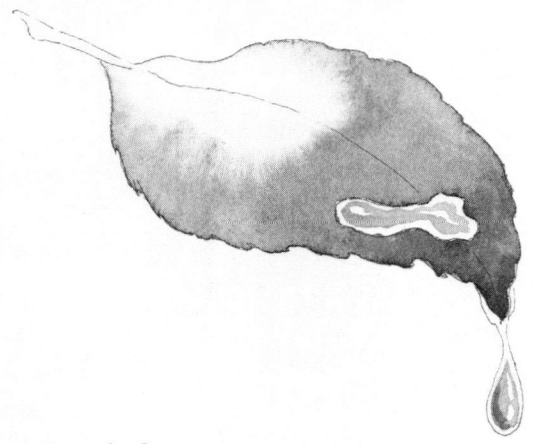

Myra and Tom's Story

"When I went back to work, Tom and I agreed to start sharing the housework," says Myra, a hospital dietitian. "Unfortunately, his idea of sharing was to take out the garbage, unload the dishwasher, and point out to me that there were dustballs under the bed or that the baby's diaper needed to be changed. If I hadn't been so exhausted all the time, I think I would have thrown something at him. Instead, I hired a cleaning service. It's cut down on the hassles, and possibly saved our marriage—or Tom's life."

Communicating: New Strategies for Dual-Income Households

Multiple Choice:

Androgyny is

    a) an ancient Roman warrior.

    b) a disease of the lower digestive tract.

    c) when an individual exhibits traits usually associated with both genders.

The correct answer is **c**. And no, it isn't icky. On the contrary, it can work out very well because few traits can or should be described as either "masculine" or "feminine." We have stereotyped ideas about the way a man or a woman should behave, but these are not based on fact. They have most of their roots in tradition and myth.

What kinds of traits do you think characterize you? The words and phrases listed below are often used to describe the way people feel or behave. Circle the ones you think apply to yourself.

1. self-reliant
2. independent
3. assertive
4. forceful
5. analytical
6. willing to risk
7. self-sufficient
8. aggressive
9. leader
10. competitive
11. ambitious
12. athletic
13. adaptable
14. conscientious
15. reliable
16. trusting
17. yielding
18. cheerful
19. shy
20. affectionate
21. loyal
22. sympathetic
23. nurturing
24. compassionate
25. tactful
26. tender
27. loves children
28. sincere

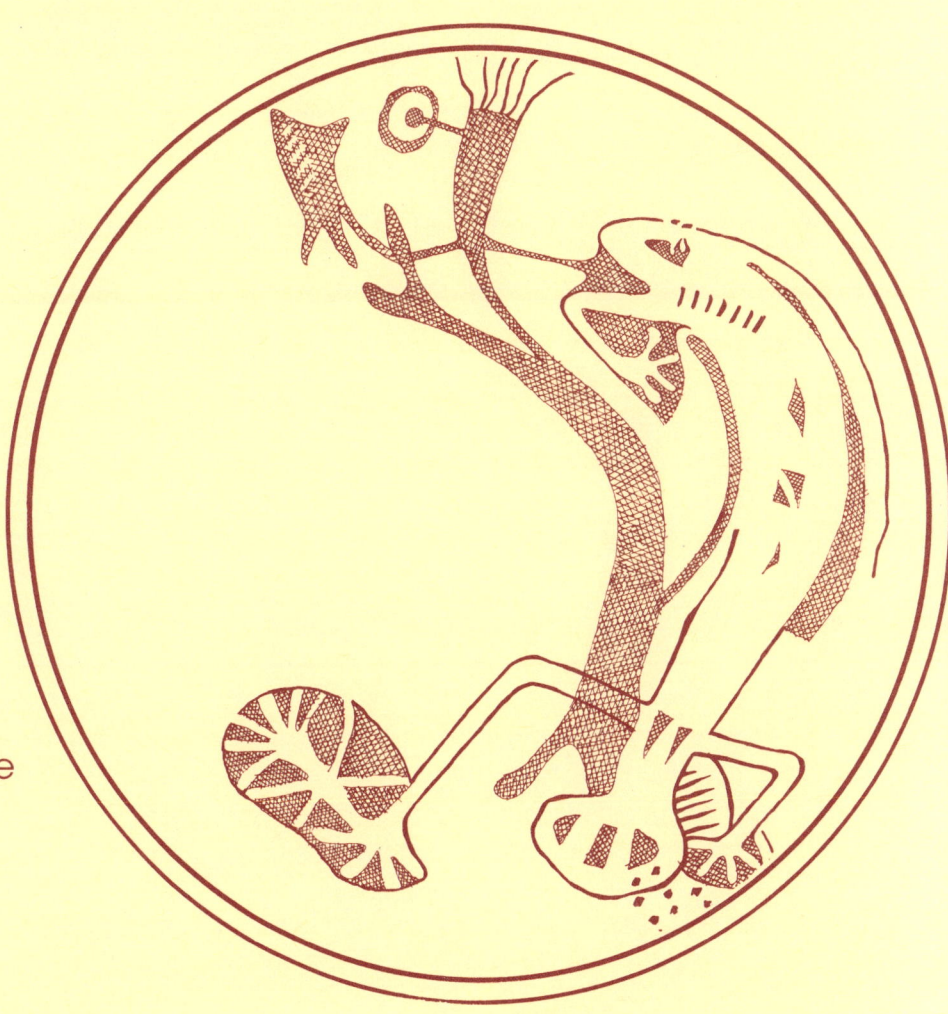

SCORE YOURSELF:

How many characteristics did you circle between numbers 1–12? _____

How many characteristics did you circle between numbers 13–16? _____

How many characteristics did you circle between numbers 17–28? _____

Numbers 1–12 are usually thought of as masculine traits; numbers 13–16 as neuter (associated with both sexes); and numbers 17–28 as feminine characteristics. It's unfortunate that these associations have been made, since we all know women can be just as independent or ambitious as men, and men are quite capable of being cheerful or loyal. How did you rate? Ideally, you should have circled traits from all three categories.

An Australian study indicates that the happiest and most successful people of both sexes exhibit both the masculine and feminine characteristics—and use them at the appropriate times. The study found that, in relationships, the couples who rated themselves happiest and who got along best both scored high in "feminine" traits like affection, sympathy, and tenderness. In the workplace, people of both sexes who were most successful exhibited such "masculine" traits as assertiveness, leadership, and self-sufficiency.

It's a shame that these traits have acquired labels that associate them with one sex or the other. They really don't have anything to do with a person's sex. Maybe they should have been called external traits and internal traits, or public traits and private traits. Things would have been less confusing that way—and less threatening, as well.

So, let's stop thinking of personality characteristics as being either masculine or feminine. Instead, consider when each should be used. Think of the so-called feminine traits as parts of your personality to use in personal relationships, or in building and maintaining relationships on the job. Who wouldn't want to have a tactful manager or a sympathetic podiatrist? The so-called masculine side of yourself, on the other hand, is put to good use in your work or task-oriented activities.

Maybe a little practice is in order. Consider the following situations, and circle the most appropriate response. Can you see how a statement that is entirely appropriate at home is inappropriate at the office, and vice versa?

AT HOME

Your spouse tells you he or she has lost his or her job because of cutbacks at the plant. Should your response be:

NURTURING: "I'm so sorry! You must feel awful. I know how much you loved your job." (plus a hug)

ANALYTICAL: "Well, you really should have seen it coming. You know sales have been down for the last few months. You'll find another job."

AT WORK

You want to correct an employee's habit of being late for work. Should you be:

NURTURING: "I know it's hard to be on time, but you really need to try harder. Is there anything I can do to help?"

ANALYTICAL: "Chris, you're burning the candle at both ends, and it's jeopardizing your job."

AT HOME

After an argument with your spouse about putting the cap on the toothpaste tube or some other trivial issue, would it be better to be:

ASSERTIVE: "I really don't want to hear any more of your accusations. They really are trivial."

TACTFUL: "Let's not blow these little things out of proportion. We're both just tired."

AT WORK

An employee misfiles an important tax report for the second time, causing the company financial and legal problems. Should you be:

ASSERTIVE: "Terry, you know better than to let something like this happen. I'd like an explanation."

TACTFUL: "It seems we have a problem with the tax report. Do you know anything about it?"

AT HOME

Your spouse re-injures a knee playing tennis in spite of warnings from the doctor. Should you be:

AGGRESSIVE: "I told you something like this would happen. Don't expect any special treatment from me."

TENDER: "Oh, you did it again! Let's get you comfortable, and then I'll call the doctor."

AT WORK

While clothes shopping on your lunch hour, you run into an employee who called in sick this morning (for the third time this month). Should you be:

AGGRESSIVE: "I'd like to see you in my office first thing tomorrow morning."

TENDER: "Oh, you must be feeling better. I hope you'll be able to come to work tomorrow."

You get the idea. Now practice writing your own responses to the following situations. After your response, indicate which trait you picked as most appropriate. Turn back to page 183 and make your choice from the list provided. Remember the formula: Masculine traits are probably more appropriate at work or in task-related activities; feminine traits at home or in building relationships.

At Home
Your spouse accidentally overdraws the family checking account.

_____

_____

At Work
Your bookkeeper accidentally overdraws the business checking account.

_____

_____

At Home
Your spouse's attempt at fixing the toilet is not entirely successful.

_____

_____

At Work
Your employee's report on the project you assigned to her is not acceptable.

_____

_____

At Home
You are tired of being criticized by your mother-in-law.

_____

_____

At Work
You are tired of being criticized by one of your clients.

_____

_____

Did you have more problems coming up with appropriate responses for work situations, or those at home? It is probably easier to label a response clearly correct or incorrect when it comes to personal relationships. The boundaries at work are a little fuzzier, since most work situations also involve relationships. As more women enter management positions, the boundaries may nearly disappear. Women are beginning to "humanize" the workplace. They tend to get things done through cooperation rather than intimidation. And that's great. If you can accomplish your job and still be cheerful, compassionate and tactful, good for you! Don't confuse compassion with passivity, though. Stand up for your rights, or what you think is right. Don't be a doormat.

As our lives become blurred with the effort of being both nurturer *and* bread-winner, it is important that both men and women learn to shift between their feminine and masculine sides when the situation calls for it. If you can learn this skill, you will probably be happier in your intimate relationships and more successful in your career or goal-oriented tasks.

Caring for Relationships

Perhaps because men are still a little reluctant to exhibit some of those "feminine" characteristics we just discussed, the care and nurturing of relationships tend to become a woman's reponsibility. Women seem to have a sixth sense about when things are not going well in a marriage, and it is important to stop when that happens and take action to correct the situation. Ideally, as men become better nurturers themselves, they will take greater leadership in this role. But to keep a marriage healthy when both partners are working outside the home, keep the following points in mind.

Talk to each other. Share your dreams, your goals and your priorities. Open communication is essential for a healthy relationship. Encourage the men in your life to develop the "feminine" side of their personalities.

Try to understand the requirements of each other's careers and how those requirements affect your relationship (where you will live, how much time the job takes, who will make more money, what sacrifices will need to be made, etc.).

Share the previous communication exercise with your partner. Discuss how important it is for *both* of you to relate to each other from your feminine sides. Review characteristics numbered 17–28 on page 183 and make an effort to communicate from that orientation. And remember, it can be just as difficult for the career woman to "shift gears" to her feminine side when she comes home from work as it is for the man.

Set aside time to be alone together. Turn back to the circle graph you drew in Chapter 8. Did you allot time for maintaining your closest relationship? If not, graph what you think might be a typical day below, being sure to make time for your mate.

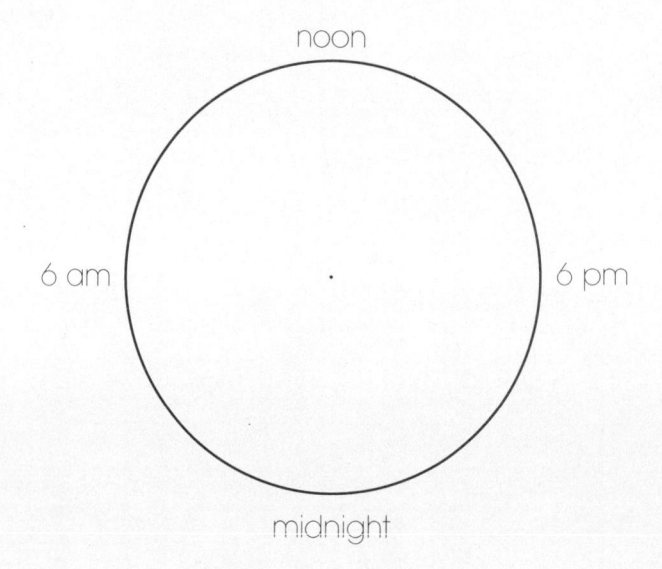

Friends: Important Relationships

When the term family is used, most people think of husbands and wives, parents and grandparents, children and grandchildren. But many people choose not to marry or have children, and yet they still lead full and satisfying lives. As their formula for happiness, they have chosen close and lasting friendships. They nurture these friendships and invest time and energy in their maintenance. Their close friends make up their "family."

So take the time to stay in touch with all the people you care about. As the old saying goes, "You have to be a friend to have a friend." A few close friends will enrich your life in good times and bad.

REFLECTIONS

CHAPTER TEN

Children & Child Care: Careful Planning Pays Off

> More than any other human relationship, overwhelmingly more, motherhood means being instantly interruptible, responsive, responsible.
> —Tillie Olsen

> Before I got married I had six theories about bringing up children; now I have six children and no theories.
> —John Wilmont
> Earl of Rochester (1647-1680)

Tom and Lupe's Story

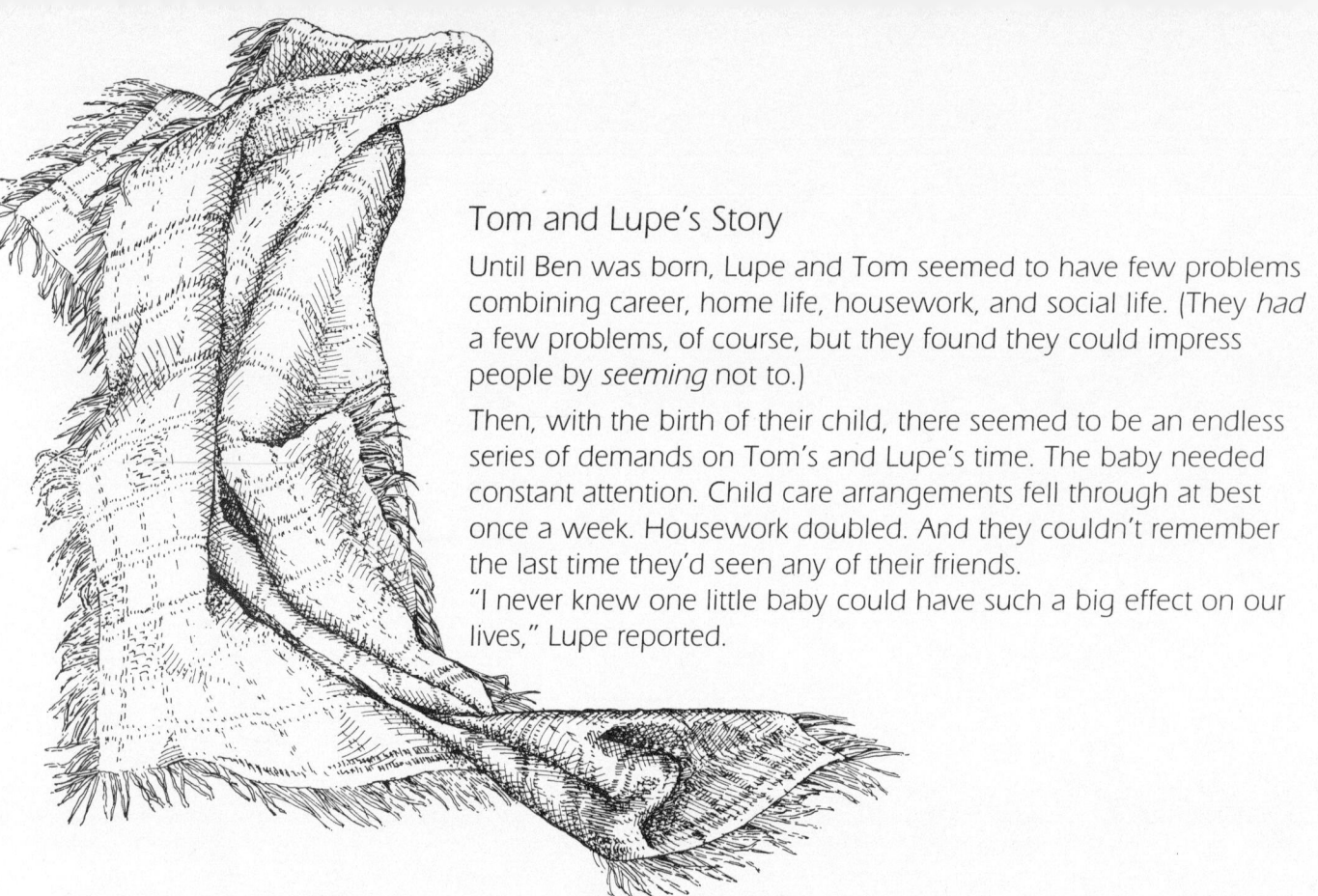

Until Ben was born, Lupe and Tom seemed to have few problems combining career, home life, housework, and social life. (They *had* a few problems, of course, but they found they could impress people by *seeming* not to.)

Then, with the birth of their child, there seemed to be an endless series of demands on Tom's and Lupe's time. The baby needed constant attention. Child care arrangements fell through at best once a week. Housework doubled. And they couldn't remember the last time they'd seen any of their friends.

"I never knew one little baby could have such a big effect on our lives," Lupe reported.

Make Your Own Choice— And Don't Feel Guilty

What Lupe and Tom know now (along with, roughly, every other parent in the world) is that having a child affects every other aspect of your life. The changes a baby makes can be wonderfully fulfilling, but many young parents are not prepared for the all-consuming demands of their new charge.

A baby must be a priority in the household and, unless you can make that kind of commitment, you may want to rethink your decision to have a child. There is, after all, no rule that says everyone should be a parent. More and more people today are finding that, perhaps to their own surprise, they find fulfillment in their jobs, in their friends or in any other arrangement that suits their own values. Unfortunately, many people still feel guilty if they do not meet the expectations of traditional "society."

It is ironic that those who *do* what they are expected to do—marry and have children—also often wrestle with guilt. They usually feel guilty about leaving their young children in order to work outside the home.

Their guilt should be easily assuaged. Recent studies indicate that children of working mothers are just as happy and well adjusted as children of women who stay at home—providing, that is, that the mother herself is happy with the choice. Feeling comfortable with your situation is most important to both you and your baby, so think carefully about the decisions you make, and then accept them. There's no need to either feel guilty or to constantly wonder whether you made the right choice.

Child Care: Problems and Possibilities

Save your energy for dealing with child care. As you learned in Chapter 2, it can be scarce, expensive, complicated, undependable or any combination of the above. But, if we all complain loudly enough and work hard enough, that may change.

Women are becoming increasingly important to American businesses, and this fact should lead to lessening of the maternity/child care dilemma in the future. Employers may become more generous with maternity and paternity leaves, and they may offer assistance to working parents, either in the form of on-site day care or financial aid to cover the costs of other child care arrangements. Other possibilities for relief include school programs for older kids, tax deductions for child care, families sharing child care tasks, or better training and pay for child care providers. Right now, though, most parents are on their own. And since there are no guarantees that the future will be better, you need to think about the kind of child care you would like to have, and then make plans accordingly.

In Chapter 2, you saw some of the grim statistics about the cost and availability of various arrangements. If you have $120 to $250 a week to spend on child care, you can have a live-in babysitter, perhaps the most desirable plan for busy families. But only about five percent of all working women can afford a full-time sitter.

A private day care school can cost from $80 to $200 per child per week. Clearly, especially if you have more than one child, this is also a costly situation. Not all of these centers are licensed, by any means, but if you can get your child into one that is, you at least have the satisfaction of knowing that the staff has been certified as pre-school teachers. Some of the best schools, though, have long waiting lists. Women have been known to apply for a spot for their child as soon as—or even before—they know they are pregnant!

Whether by choice or necessity, about 40% of working parents leave their children in family day care centers.[1] These are usually run by a woman who cares for two to five pre-schoolers in her own home. Costs range from about $40 to $70 per week per child. Some of these day care homes are excellent, but others are less satisfactory.

For a single mother with two children, though, a minimum child care payment of $80 a week is often out of reach. Thousands of these women resort to a desperate juggling act, in which children may be shifted from a neighbor's house to a friend's house to a relative's house every day. The more complicated the arrangement, the better the chance that it will fall through, leaving the mother to make frantic last-minute phone calls, or to miss a day of work. These women, understandably, are among the least satisfied and most stressed in the country.

Happily combining parenting and career takes careful planning. This stage of your life, the career-planning stage, is not too soon to start thinking about it. Will you or your partner be able to take time off from your job to stay home with your young child? Will you be able to afford the kind of outside help you would feel most comfortable with? Is one child enough, or do you want a bigger family? Do you want to have children at all? The following exercises should help you clarify your thoughts and explore your options.

Child Care: What's Your Ideal?

As a member of the new generation of working parents, you may be in a position to make some changes in the kind and quality of child care now available. What kind of care do you think there should be? Don't just compare the services you've heard about. Think about the **possibilities.** Describe your ideal child care situation for:

Your one-year-old: _____
_____
_____

Your three-year-old: _____
_____
_____

Your six-year-old: _____
_____
_____

Your eleven-year-old: _____
_____
_____

Do facilities for that kind of care exist in your community? Check them out. If they are available, how much do they cost? If they aren't, what might be done to create these services?

Situation	Where they are available	Cost

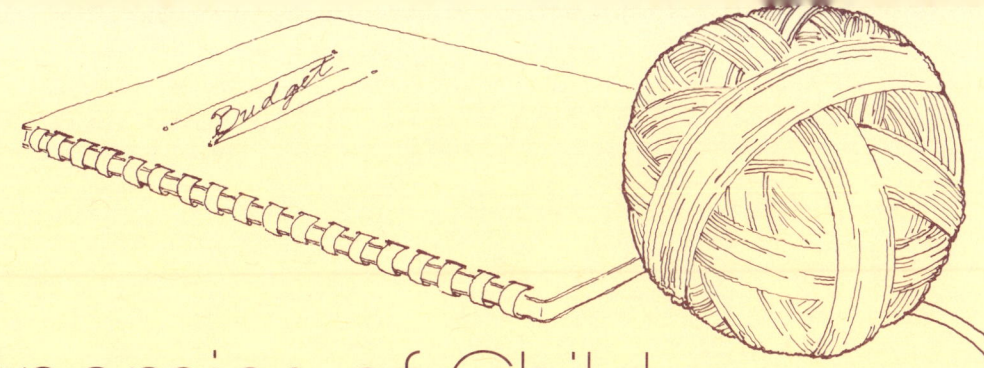

The Economics of Child Care

As you've seen, providing care for a small child can be an expensive proposition. Like most parents, though, you will probably want to find the best care available for your baby. To do this, you may have to make sacrifices in other areas of your life. As things now stand, even if you are willing to do without all but the barest necessities for yourself, your options for quality child care may be limited if you do not earn enough money. It's a bad situation, one we should all be working to correct. But, today, it is the norm. Let's see how the income levels of three single parents affect their children and themselves.

John, Jacque and Joya are single parents living in the same apartment building. Each has two children, ages three and six. The three pay the same amount of rent ($350 a month, utilities included) for their two-bedroom, one-bath apartments. They all drive similar economy cars and drive about the same distance to work. They live frugally, buying most clothing on sale and eating most meals at home. The fixed expenses in their budgets include:

Housing	$350
Transportation	$180
Clothing	$ 75
Food & Sundries	$200

John works as a bank teller and earns $6.00 an hour. His gross pay is $12,120 a year, or $1,010 a month. His take-home pay is $875 a month.

As an administrative assistant to the president of a small construction company, Jacque earns $9.00 an hour for an annual income of $18,720, or $1,560 a month. Her take-home pay is $1,300 a month.

Joya is a computer service technician earning $15.00 an hour. Her gross pay is $31,200 a year, or $2,600 a month. Her take-home pay is $2,000 a month.

Below, make up a sample monthly budget for each person. Start by subtracting fixed expenses from take-home pay to see how much discretionary income you have to work with.

	John	Jacque	Joya
Housing	$350	$350	$350
Transportation	$180	$180	$180
Clothing	$ 75	$ 75	$ 75
Food	$200	$200	$200
Entertainment			
Furnishings			
Health care			
Child care (from previous exercise)			
Savings			
Miscellaneous			
TOTAL	$875	$1,300	$2,000

What options does John have for child care? _____

What options does Jacque have? _____

How about Joya? _____

What arrangements might the three parents make together to care for all their children cooperatively?

If you could see into the future and knew you were going to be a single parent, what could you do **now** to assure that your family would have a more comfortable and secure life?

Stress and the Working Parent

Earlier in this chapter, we said that single parents are under more stress than most other Americans. But this is not necessarily just because they are single parents. Consider John's, Jacque's and Joya's situation one more time. Which person do you think is most likely to suffer from stress? (Hint: Stress often results from the feeling that you have little control over your life.)

Joya's salary allows her to have the kind of child care she chooses for her children. In addition, she can be somewhat flexible about her work hours, so she can usually make arrangements to attend her children's school programs, or take them to the doctor. Jacque's job pays less well, but still gives her some feeling of control. She is expected to be at work during business hours, but can make arrangements with her boss to take an early or late lunch when she needs to do something for or with her kids. John's income gives him few choices about the kind of child care he can provide. And his job at the bank is not at all flexible.

Single parents are not the only people who suffer from stress, by any means. Anyone trying to balance career and family life is susceptible. Women, especially, find their days become so crammed with tasks and responsibilities that there is no way to get it all done. Then there are the conflicting responsibilities: Your child wakes up with a fever of 103 degrees Fahrenheit the day you have an important presentation to make at the office. Do you stay home and shirk your work responsibilities? Or do you go to work and feel like a rotten mother? It is interesting to note that fathers, as a rule, do not have the same kinds of conflicts. Few people ever suggest that *they* should stay home with a sick child.

Women, however, are still trying to live up to the traditional image of motherhood. Women were led to believe that being a mother was an all-encompassing task, and that they were entirely responsible for the physical, social and emotional well-being of their youngsters. It is difficult to take seriously the notion that a child's psyche could be permanently damaged because her mother didn't cut the crusts off the peanut butter sandwiches taken to school, but some people actually held notions like that.

Even though we know better now, women still tend to get bad cases of the "shoulds" and "ought tos" when they return to work after having a child. And this, too, can lead to stress. It doesn't come just from being busy. *All* working mothers are busy. Some control stress by having realistic expectations of how much they can do in any one sphere of their lives. They don't try to do everything themselves. Many find that their careers have a great deal to do with the amount of stress in their family lives.

On the surface, it may seem that the less responsibility your job entails, the less stressful it will be. But, actually, the opposite is true. The more responsibility you have at work, the more *control* you will have. (There's that word again.) And, as we've said before, a feeling of control is a key in limiting stress.

Take Control and Plan

So one good way to deal with stress is to be a leader in your company. This can work in several ways. You will probably make more money in a leadership position, and this will give you more control over the way you live. You can choose the kind of child care you like best. Maybe you can hire other people to perform chores for you, leaving you more time for your family.

In a position of power, you will also have more flexibility to decide when and where you will work. If a child is sick, you may be able to call in and say you will work at home that day. You will almost certainly be able to adjust your hours to attend a child's choral recital or soccer match.

And, finally, if you are in a decision-making position, you may be able to steer company policy in a direction that's more compatible with parenting in general. You may be able to make combining career and family life less stressful for all parents.

Other stress-reducing or problem-sharing strategies include:

Working at home. We've already discussed the benefits of an in-home office. You may have to set up some strict rules about not being disturbed if you are to get any work done, but this arrangement can be efficient.

Working four days a week. Some couples arrange to work four ten-hour days each week, with one person working Monday through Thursday, and the other Tuesday through Friday. That leaves just three days when neither parent is at home.

Sharing the workload. There is a lot of talk about men sharing household responsibilities, but women still end up doing most of the work. It doesn't have to be this way. If you marry wisely (be sure to discuss this *ahead* of time), you can arrange to share the chores that go along with caring for a family. Maybe one of you will do most of the cooking, while the other cares for the children.

Sharing with another family. Successful cooperative arrangements involve sharing meals or child care, or exchanging services. For example, if your friend is an ace at yard work, but can't take care of a car, and your talents are just the reverse, you can set up an exchange system that works out well for everyone.

Working different shifts. Couples who feel strongly that one parent should be at home most of the time sometimes arrange to work different shifts. The difficulty here is that husband and wife see very little of each other during the week.

Can you think of other strategies?

_____
_____
_____
_____

Most young couples report that, ideally, they would like to have two children. When the first baby comes, they are confident that all will go well. And, in spite of the problems, they find their lives enriched by the child. Then comes the moment of truth: Should they have that second baby? Managing a household with two children is more complicated than making arrangements for a family with a single child. With two children on the scene, you are faced with some tough choices: Should you take time out from your career to care for your young family? Or should you stay on the job?

This is a choice every working mother must make for herself. Either way, there are things she will have to give up. If she decides to keep her job, she may miss such events as seeing her baby take its first steps or hearing its first words. She may have less energy for her spouse and children at the end of a long day.

Taking Time Out

If you decide to stay home for a period of years, on the other hand, the family may suffer financially. Or you may find it difficult to make up for lost time when you go back to work. Some careers have definite "career ladders." This means that, in order to be considered successful, you must reach certain levels of promotion or responsibility within a certain time frame. Business management usually works this way. So does becoming a partner in a law or investment firm. Taking time out in fields like these can quite possibly take you out of the running for top positions. In other fields, a sabbatical is more acceptable. If you think you would like to be able to stay home when your children are young, you might consider careers in which your skills are more important than your record of promotions.

Some careers that don't have a prescribed career ladder are:

- Word processing
- Graphic designing
- Sales
- Engineering
- Plumbing
- Computer programming

Can you think of others? List some below.

_____   _____

_____   _____

_____   _____

_____   _____

Full-Time Parenting?

Being at home to watch your children grow and learn can be more rewarding than any paid career. (Assuming you *could* support your family if you had to.) Again, though, there will be trade-offs. If you agree with most of the statements which follow, you might be happier as a full-time parent than you would be trying to hold down an outside job while your children are young.

	Agree	Dis-agree	Don't Know
1. I enjoy a picnic as much as lunch at a fancy restaurant.			
2. I like the challenge of living well on a limited budget.			
3. I wouldn't miss the stimulation of a work environment.			
4. I'd rather entertain guests at home than have an evening on the town.			
5. It's not important to me to own my own home.			
6. I don't need money to make me feel successful.			
7. Expensive vacations can wait until the kids are grown.			
8. It would be just as stimulating for me to teach my child to read as it would be to develop a new program at work.			
9. It would be just as exciting for me to spend a day at the zoo with the kids as it would be to present an important project at work.			
10. I think a parent should always be home for a sick child.			
11. I believe that no one can care for a child as well as its parent.			
12. I wouldn't be envious if a co-worker got the promotion I'd been waiting for while I was home with my children.			
13. I wouldn't miss daily conversations with other adults.			
14. I'd rather send my children to public schools than private schools.			
15. I have hobbies and other interests to keep me stimulated while I'm away from my career.			
16. My spouse and friends will support my decision to be a full-time parent.			
17. I don't need to be employed to feel important.			
18. For a few years, I can gladly sacrifice my own interests for the sake of my children.			
19. My children do not need to attend expensive camps or own costly gadgets.			
20. I find cooking on a budget more challenging than preparing a gourmet meal.			
21. I'd rather raise my child than raise my salary.			
22. My maternal instincts are stronger than my material instincts.			

Decide for Yourself

Whether you elect to stay home with your children full time, work part time while parenting, or balance a full-time career with raising your children, remember that, "Every parent is a working parent." You are carrying out an important job and have every right to be proud of your accomplishments.

We've talked a lot about balancing career and family life because most people say that they want the whole package. We don't, however, mean to indicate that EVERYONE wants, or SHOULD want, to live this way. Today your options are wide open. You may get so wrapped up in your career that you don't have time to get married. You may find satisfaction in a circle of close friends rather than in a traditional family. Perhaps you will marry and you and your spouse will decide that you cannot, or do not wish to, make children the kind of priority they need to be, and so elect not to have a child. The list goes on: You might want to support a cause instead of a family, or you may decide to care for someone else's children. Perhaps you will live in a cooperative environment with other people's parents and children, as well as people your own age. Whatever you decide, you are sure to learn that there is no shortage of people, whatever their age, who need your love and care.

The key to having a satisfying life is to live it the way YOU want to. If you are honestly determined to have a spouse, six kids, three dogs and a full-time career, you just might be able to pull it off. If you mix career and family just because you think that's expected of you, you will almost certainly be dissatisfied with your life.

Decide for yourself the kind of life you want. Your goals and values may change as you get older, so you will need to re-evaluate the situation from time to time. But it's not too soon to begin planning for your future. The next chapter will help you get started.

> It is not best that we should all think alike; it is difference of opinion which makes horse races.
> —Mark Twain

REFLECTIONS

Chapter Eleven

Your Own Strategic Plan for Mixing Career & Family

There is only one success—to be able to spend your life in your own way.
—Ben Sweetland

If you don't know where you are going, you will probably end up somewhere else.

I think somehow we learn who we really are and then live with that decision.
—Eleanor Roosevelt

Planning Your Future

If you've read the last ten chapters, you know that your future holds thousands of promises— and just as many problems. There are two ways to deal with problems and opportunities: You can shut your eyes, cross your fingers and hope for the best. Or you can make a plan.

Planning can help you make the most of your opportunities. And, while no one gets through life without problems, it can minimize the effects they have on you and your family.

Most people don't know how to go about career planning. But it's been going on for years, and it is a wise thing to do. Today you need to expand the traditional process. You need to take into account all the issues we've discussed. This chapter will help you write your best plan for a successful career and family life.

First, though, you need to define success in your own terms. Usually we think about success in relation to careers. But you also need to decide what would make you feel successful in your personal and family life, and what would make you feel successful in your community, or in the larger world. Take some time to think about it, because these are questions *only you* can answer. Trying to live up to someone else's idea of success is an empty and frustrating experience.

Consider, for example, "The Woman in the Gray Flannel Suit," one of the many women who entered the business world in the 1970s with hopes of succeeding—in male terms. She was immediately recognizable by her uniform, a gray or navy skirted suit, button-down shirt, bow-tie, and low-heeled pumps. This outfit, supposedly, would make her seem like "one of the boys." She tried her best to act like her male colleagues, too, and went to great lengths to make people forget there was anything feminine about her. While her male co-workers could display photos of their children in their offices, "The Woman in the Gray Flannel Suit" could not: Someone might suspect that she was really a woman, after all, and, therefore, not serious about her career.

Sadly, few people were fooled. Men, it seems, are usually better at being men than women are. Even when she did "succeed," "The Woman in the Gray Flannel Suit" often found her victory meaningless. Trying to live by someone else's rules, she gave up many of the things that were important to her.

Imagine what would make you a success in your own eyes. Then, in the spaces below, briefly describe what you would like to accomplish in different areas of your life. Is one area more important to you than the others? How would you define success for yourself in relation to:

Work/career _____

_____

_____

Family/friends/relationships _____

_____

_____

Personal happiness _____

_____

_____

Community/society _____

_____

_____

Clarifying Your Thoughts on Family Life

How did you define success in terms of family life? The following quiz should help you clarify your feelings about child care and home life. Choose or write a statement below that most accurately reflects your own thoughts. But don't limit yourself to what you think is realistic. Go for your *ideal* situation. If you keep in mind the kind of family life you would find most fulfilling, you will be in a better position to choose a career that will fit your needs.

1. I believe that
   a. A mother should always be home with her children.
   b. A parent should always be home with the children.
   c. A mother can work outside the home 10–30 hours a week.
   d. A mother can work outside the home full time, 40 hours a week.
   e. A mother can work at a demanding career, 50–60 hours a week.
   f. A mother can/should _____
   _____.

2. My ideal child care situation would be
   a. Staying home with my children, not working outside the home.
   b. Having a parent (or relative) not working outside the home stay home with the children.
   c. A part-time nursery school or private child care arrangement.
   d. A full-time public pre-school.
   e. A full-time sitter in my home.
   f. Your own statement: _____
   _____.

3. I believe
   a. A pregnant woman should quit her job and stay home at least until the children enter school.
   b. A parent should stay home with children at least until they enter school.
   c. A mother or father should stop working until their child is old enough to enter nursery school.
   d. A woman should take all the maternity leave she is allowed before returning to work.
   e. A woman should get back to work as soon as she is able following the birth of her child.
   f. Your own statement: _____
   _____

4. If both parents work outside the home full time, I believe
   a. The woman should be responsible for the majority of parenting and housework.
   b. Both parents should share parenting and household tasks equally.
   c. The parent with the less demanding or more flexible job should assume more responsibility for parenting and housework.
   d. With proper time management, a mother can juggle career, parenting, and household responsibilities.
   e. Outside domestic help is needed to meet all the requirements of parenting and housework.
   f. Your own statement: _____
   _____

5. If one parent works full time and the other works half time, I believe
   a. The woman should be responsible for the majority of parenting and housework.
   b. Both parents should share parenting and household tasks equally.
   c. The parent working the least number of hours should do more of the parenting and housework.
   d. With proper time management, a mother can juggle career, parenting, and household responsibilities.
   e. Outside domestic help is desirable to meet all the requirements of parenting and housework.
   f. Your own statement:_____
   _____

6. When a child is sick
   a. Its mother should stay home from work.
   b. A parent should stay home from work.
   c. Schedules should be juggled, or relatives can help.
   d. A mother should take the sick child to the sitter even if she doesn't want to.
   e. A trained sitter/nurse should be called.
   f. Your own statement:_____
   _____

7. The ideal time for a couple to start a family is
   a. Anytime, since the woman should be a full-time care-giver.
   b. Anytime, as long as one parent can be a full-time care-giver.
   c. When they have completed their education and started their careers.
   d. When they are financially secure and their careers are in full swing.
   e. When they are firmly established in their careers.
   f. Your own statement:_____
   _____

8. I feel a woman can mix career and family by
   a. Making motherhood her full-time career.
   b. Sharing responsibilities equally with a supportive spouse.
   c. Working 40 hours a week and carefully managing her time.
   d. Working part time outside the home.
   e. Working at a career with flexible hours.
   f. Your own statement:_____
   _____

9. I would like to have
   a. Three or more children.
   b. Two children.
   c. One child.
   d. No children.
   e. More time to make a decision.
   f. Your own statement:_____
   _____

Your statements will serve as a guide to your ideal situation. As in anything, you may change your mind in the coming years, so go back and re-take this quiz from time to time. But refer to this list as you complete the exercises in this chapter.

Evaluating Your Financial Needs

As you learned in Chapter 3, people value money for many different reasons. Turn back to page 53 and review your responses to the quiz. List the two categories in which you scored highest below.

_____

_____

Now consider what your financial needs will be when you have the number of children you said you would like to have in the previous exercise. Assume that you are a single parent. Turn back to the sample budgets you made for Melody on pages 44 to 46 and use them as a guide. Which budget do you think would best meet your needs? Be sure to add any discretionary costs for items you indicated you would like to have in the previous exercise (a housekeeper, a full-time sitter, etc.). Write your monthly budget below.

TOTAL MONTHLY PAYMENTS

ITEM	AMOUNT	DESCRIPTION
Rent or mortgage	_____	_____
		_____
Utilities	_____	_____
Insurance	_____	_____
Transportation	_____	_____
Food	_____	_____
		_____
Child care	_____	_____
Clothing	_____	_____
Entertainment	_____	_____
Medical	_____	_____
Household help	_____	_____
Vacations	_____	_____
Gifts and contributions	_____	_____
TOTAL PER MONTH	_____ (a)	_____

Find the gross monthly income required. For this example figure that you will have 20% of your salary withheld for taxes and benefits. In short, divide your net income requirement (a) by 80%.

_____ (a) ÷ .80 = _____ (b)

Multiply your total monthly budget by 12 to determine how much income you need to take home each year.

12 × $_____ (b) = $_____ (c) annual income required

Divide that figure by 2080 hours to determine how much you would need to earn per hour at a full-time job to support this budget.

_____ (c) ÷ $\frac{2080 \text{ hours/year}}{}$ = _____ (d)
hourly wage
required at a
full-time job

(As you do your career research to find your net income which is your take-home pay, deduct an average of 20% from the listed salaries to account for taxes and social security.)

Investigating Possible Careers

Now it's time to consider possible careers. Choose one that appeals to you, and then answer the following questions about it. The first 12 questions, taken from *Choices*, are standard for any career research model. The others have been added to help you see how compatible the career would be with raising a family.

To find specific information about the field you are investigating, see the career section of your school or public library. Two exceptionally good sources are *The Occupational Outlook Handbook* and the *Dictionary of Occupational Titles*, or DOT.

Job title _____

1. List specific activities to be performed on the job. (Some examples would be: "Carpenter—measuring, sawing, hammering, sanding. Lawyer—writing, interviewing clients, giving speeches in courtroom.")

   _____
   _____
   _____
   _____

2. What is the job environment? Is the job done indoors or outdoors? In a large office? In a noisy factory?

   _____
   _____

3. What rewards does the job provide? High salary? Convenient hours? Emotional satisfaction? Pleasant surroundings? Adventure?

   _____
   _____
   _____

4. Why would this job be particularly satisfying to *you*? Review your values, interests, and life goals for guidance here.

   _____
   _____
   _____

5. How much training or education is required? Where could you get it? (Some examples are: a four-year degree from a university, six months at a business or trade school.) If possible, try to find a specific school or place where you could receive the training you would need. Not all colleges offer degrees in architecture, marine biology, and so forth.

_____
_____
_____
_____

6. Are there any physical limitations? If so, what are they? (Strength requirements, health requirements, 20/20 vision, etc.)

_____
_____
_____

7. What is the approximate starting salary for the job? Mid-career salary?

_____
_____

8. What is the projected outlook for this occupation? Will there be many jobs available when you are ready to enter the job market? Or are there few openings and much competition?

_____
_____
_____
_____

9. What skills and talents are required?

_____
_____
_____
_____

10. How can you begin today to prepare for this career?

_____
_____
_____
_____

11. What classes do you need to take in school to pursue this career?

_____
_____

12. Where would you find employment in this job in your community or state?

_____
_____
_____

Now let's focus on how this career meets your parenting requirements

13. Would this job meet your economic requirements? Use the following equations to evaluate your options.

    According to my budget on page 209, I need to earn $_____ (a) per year. *Figure (c) from page 209.*

    Working full time (40 hours per week) I would have to earn $_____ (b) per hour.

    $$\$_____ \text{ (a)} \div 2080 = \$_____ \text{ (b)}$$

    Working half time (20 hours per week) I would have to earn $_____ (c) per hour.

    $$\$_____ \text{ (a)} \div 1040 = \$_____ \text{ (c)}$$

    The average full time salary for this career is $_____ (d) per year.

    Therefore the average hourly rate for this career is $_____ (e) per hour.

    $$\$_____ \text{ (d)} \div 2080 = \$_____ \text{ (e)}$$

    Could I support myself and my family on the average salary of this career working full time?

             Yes   No

    Could I support myself and my family on the average salary of this career if I only worked half time?

             Yes   No

    $$\$_____ \text{ (e)} \times 1040 = \$_____$$

    Here is another way to look at average salary and economic sufficiency.

    How many hours per week would I have to work at this career to support my family?

    $$\underbrace{\$_____}_{\substack{\text{annual income} \\ \text{requirement}}} \text{(a)} \div \underbrace{_____}_{\substack{\text{average} \\ \text{career} \\ \text{salary}}} \text{(d)} \times 40 \text{ hrs./wk.} = _____$$

    Would this schedule fit in with your plans for parenting and family life? If not, can you think of alternatives?

    _____
    _____
    _____

14. Turn back again to your list of child care priorities on page 206. How flexible must your career be to accommodate them?

    _____
    _____

15. How flexible are the hours in this career?

    _____
    _____

16. Are part-time jobs available in this field?
_____
_____

17. Would it be possible to freelance your skills in this field? How?
_____
_____
_____

18. Could you eventually work as a consultant in this profession? How?
_____
_____
_____

19. Do any entrepreneurial opportunities exist here? What?
_____
_____

20. Could you transfer experience gained here to another field? Which fields?
_____
_____

21. If there are different specialities in this profession, which would be likely to have the most flexible hours?
_____
_____

22. Does this field usually provide for maternity leave?   Yes   No   Don't know

23. What is the average length of maternity leave in this industry? _____

24. In this career would taking a few years off to raise your children hurt your chances of being in line for promotions or salary increases when you go back to work?

    Yes   No   Don't know

25. Is it important for you to stay on the "fast track"? Does this career have a "career ladder"?

    Yes   No   Undecided

26. Does this career meet your requirements for flexibility?   Yes   No

27. Does this career meet your income requirements?   Yes   No

Use this 27-question research model whenever you evaluate a career. It will help you not only to focus on the demands and satisfactions of the work but also on how the career will meet your personal and family needs.

Getting There From Here

Hortensia's Story

When she was sixteen years old, Hortensia decided she would like to be an accountant. She enjoyed working with numbers and, after some career research, Hortensia found that this field offered both high pay and options for the flexible hours she would need when she had a family. A born planner, Hortensia decided to list yearly goals, starting immediately, for getting where she wanted to be professionally within the next ten years. Her educational/professional chart looked like this:

Age 16: Do well in math classes
Have informational interviews with accountants
Begin sending for college catalogs

Age 17: Take more math
Visit some college campuses
Take SAT

Age 18: Apply to colleges of choice
Continue math

Age 19: Complete first year of college
Talk with counselors, professors

Age 20: Continue to do well in college accounting program
Serve on school committee working with professional accountants

Age 21: Get into honors program in college accounting program
Begin to research possible employers

Age 22: Interview with desirable employers
Graduate with honors
Join professional organization

Age 23: Accept entry-level position with well-known public accounting firm
Take class on preparation for CPA exam

Age 24: Sit for CPA exam
Continue to work and learn on the job

Age 25: Receive CPA certificate
Take class in setting up business

Age 26: Set up accounting practice at home

Of course, it is impossible to plan for all of the contingencies in life. Hortensia knew that her plan was more of a guide than a blueprint, and that she would want to or need to make adjustments along the way. At the same time, she believed in the saying, "If you don't know where you're going, you'll probably end up somewhere else." Hortensia knew the value of planning.

Now it's your turn. First decide on a goal, and enter it at **year ten** on the chart below. Then try to plan "backwards." What would you need to do in years one through nine to arrive at your ten-year goal? Write in your interim goals.

Your age today_____

Year One_____
_____
_____

Year Two_____
_____
_____

Year Three_____
_____
_____

Year Four_____
_____
_____

Year Five_____
_____
_____

Year Six_____
_____
_____

Year Seven_____
_____
_____

Year Eight_____
_____
_____

Year Nine_____
_____
_____

Year Ten_____
_____
_____

Bringing In Your Partner

If you stick to your plan, you should be able to take care of your family even if you are a single parent. Ideally, though, you will have someone to share the pleasures and responsibilities. It will help if you and your partner have the same ideas about child care and housework. Do you? Have your mate take the same parenting quiz you did. Do you have any major disagreements about the way you would like to operate your family? If so, can you find solutions that are agreeable to you both? Talk it out. This is one area in which it is vital that you and your partner be in basic agreement.

Keeping Your Life in Balance

If you think *making* your plan was hard work, wait until you try *living* it! With so much going on, so many demands on your time and attention, it's easy to get off balance. You'll need to remind yourself constantly that, while you can't have or do everything, you can have or do the things that are most important. It's a good idea to review your circle chart on a regular basis to see if you are neglecting some spheres of your life. Review and re-evaluate your priorities, too, to help keep things in perspective, or to guide you in making changes when life doesn't seem as satisfying as you think it should.

Keep in mind, too, that there are situations in life you just can't control. Not all outcomes can be anticipated, not all situations stay the same and not all choices are final. Sometimes you just need to "go with the flow," be as flexible as you can be and use your skills and experiences to make the best of what may not be an ideal situation.

Finally, be decisive. Make your best choices concerning your career and family life, and don't look back. Let go of the things you decided not to do, and get on with living the life you've chosen.

Before you get started, though, there's one more important and rewarding aspect of any well-balanced life. Read on.

REFLECTIONS

Chapter Twelve

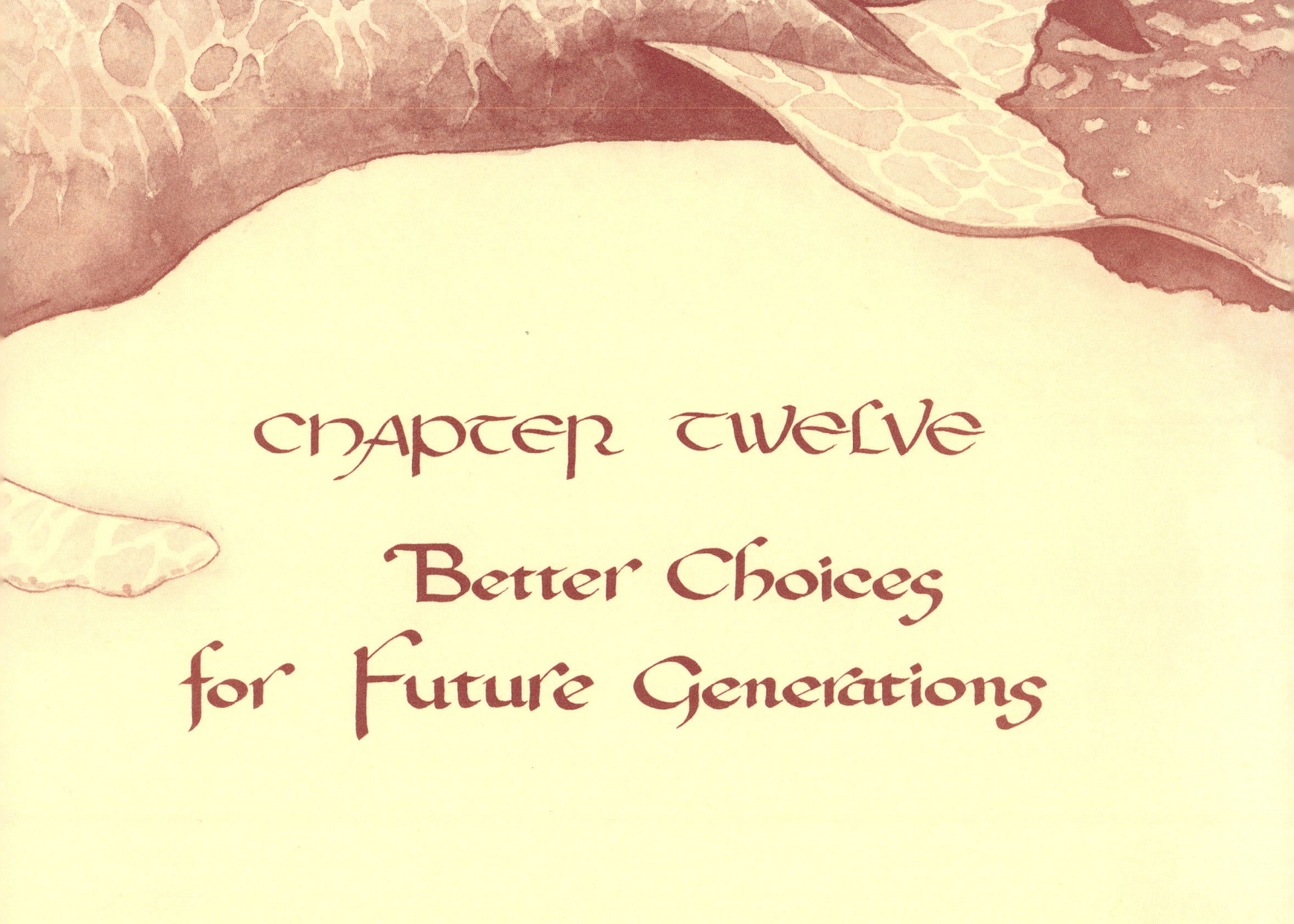

Better Choices for Future Generations

I like the dreams of the future better
than the history of the past.
—Thomas Jefferson

Never grow a wishbone, daughter,
Where your backbone ought to be.
—Clementine Paddleford

Emma Neezer-Scrooge's Story (continued)

In the weeks after her visit from the spirits, Emma Neezer-Scrooge made substantial changes in her life. She and Tim discussed their marriage, their children, and their household responsibilities. They talked about their finances and took a close look at their budget. And they considered their respective jobs, and how the whole package fit together. They decided they could afford to have a cleaning service once a week to help with the heavy cleaning, and Tim agreed to get more involved in parenting and daily household chores. Both Emma and Tim found they were spending time at unimportant activities they could easily give up. Emma asked Roberta Cratchit for more flexible hours at work and, since Emma was a valued employee, Roberta agreed.

The Neezer-Scrooge family began to spend more time together, and their lives were less frantic and more enjoyable than they had been. But Emma couldn't stop thinking about her dream. Once she had dismissed all the mythical women from her mind, she wanted to replace them. She wanted to know about the *real* lives of women, past and present. She looked at her own young daughter, Emma Jr., and wondered what her life would be like. Emma began to do some research. You already know what she found. If you've forgotten, turn back to Chapter 2. The present lives of many women are, to say the least, not what they should be.

While Emma had worked hard for all that she accomplished, she never realized how tenuous her position in the world was. She began to get angry. Was it *fair* that millions of women and children lived in poverty while the fathers of those children took no financial responsibility for them? Was it *right* that women worked as hard and as long as men for about two-thirds the pay? Isn't the welfare of children something *everyone* should be concerned about?

As she continued her research, Emma learned that there has actually been some improvement in women's lives. She felt tears well up in her eyes as she read about thousands of women, working alone and together, who had lost their jobs or gone to jail in an effort to obtain what seemed like *extremely* basic rights for their sex: the right to vote, the right to be educated and allowed into the professions, and the right to be paid equitably for their labor.

Much to her own surprise, Emma found herself envying these women. They may not have made much money, but they made something of great value: *They made a difference.* Emma was grateful that she had a good job and a wonderful family, but she vowed that she would make an effort to do something *more* with her life. She would work to see that Emma Jr., didn't have to fight for equal pay or maternity leave or the kind of care she wanted for her children.

She remembered a slogan she'd seen posted in her older sister's bedroom back in the 60s: "If you're not part of the solution," it said, "You're part of the problem." Emma decided then and there which side she was going to be on. The world had given her more than it gave most women, and Emma would give something back.

Sharing and Giving Something Back

We don't mean to sound preachy. Like Emma, most women have worked extremely hard for everything they have received in this world. Young women today feel entitled—and they *are*. You have a perfect right to expect equal treatment in everything from education to career opportunities to retirement benefits. But it's the sad truth that you probably won't get them. For every one of you who does, dozens of others will remain overworked, underpaid and unsure of where to turn for help.

What to do? There seem to be two schools of thought: the "Every Woman for Herself" school, and the "We're All in this Together" school. Up to a certain point, we are all responsible for our own lives. Most of this book has been about what you can do to give yourself and your family the best chance for success in the world. We think of this, though, as an *interim* measure. Although society is changing, permanent improvement in the way women and children live will not come until the changes are institutionalized. As of this writing, the kinds of support that would make life easier for *all* American families are not in place. And they won't be, without a concerted effort from the people who stand to benefit most from change.

The questions *you* must now ask yourself are these: "Do I want things to be this difficult for future generations? For my *own* children? How will I explain to them in later years why I did nothing to make the situation better?"

Acting for social change can be some of the most satisfying work you'll ever do. (The problem most of you will encounter is finding the time, but there are ways to get around that, too.)

> As Emma Neezer-Scrooge explained her involvement, "I thought a long time about what kind of mark I'd like to leave on the world—how I'd like my children to remember me. And I decided it wasn't enough to leave the family silver or a well-managed stock portfolio. I wanted my children to say that their mom helped *change* things. She set an *example*. She was someone they could be proud of."
>
> As she got involved, Emma sometimes saw herself as part of a proud line of brave women continuing the fight for equality. She thought of Mary Wollstonecraft, Susan B. Anthony, Elizabeth Cady Stanton, Margaret Sanger, Sojourner Truth, Emma Goldman, Alice Paul, Fanny Lou Hamer, Simone de Beauvoir, Shirley Chisholm, Betty Friedan, Geraldine Ferraro, Sally Ride, Joan Benoit and all the others, and liked to imagine her own name in conjunction with theirs.
>
> Some years after her dream, Emma Neezer-Scrooge was elected to the Congress of the United States, where she fought steadfastly to make life better for all her constituents.

But there are other ways to participate....

Authority and Power

Lena's Story

As a store manager for a chain of retail toy stores, Lena developed a reputation for creative marketing and high sales. She was soon promoted to marketing director and went to work in corporate headquarters where, again, she worked her magic, this time on a national scale. Lena climbed the corporate ladder and became the first woman president of the company.

She almost turned the promotion down. "I always had mixed feelings about power and authority," Lena said. "Maybe that's because so many people have used their power to do negative things. I just didn't want to be associated with them. But then it occurred to me that *I* could use *my* power to change all the things I'd found wrong with the company. I could make sure that the toys we carried were positive influences on children's lives. I discontinued all lines that promoted violence. In addition, I could see that more women were given a fair chance at promotions, and that hours be made more flexible for everyone. One of the first things I did was to set up a committee to start plans for an on-site day care center. I'm proud of the way I've used my power. I'm looking for more ways to use it!"

In 1980, women held 318 of 7,783 top jobs in major American institutions. That's about 4.1%.[1] And that's not a lot. Women have little to say about corporate power in America. This is due partly to discrimination and partly to the fact that women have only recently entered the work force in numbers approaching those of men. In addition, many women share Lena's early thoughts about power. They tend to concentrate on its negative uses, while overlooking the force it can be for good.

This is especially unfortunate because the philosophy of most companies, as expressed in their employment policies, tends to be the philosophy of their chief executive officer. When most CEOs are males, the issues of most concern to women tend to be overlooked.

So, if *you* can have a decision-making role at work, *you* will be in a good position to help all parents and their families. Not everyone wants to be in a position of power and authority, of course. But give the idea some thought. Don't just assume that you couldn't achieve a position that appeals to you. Set your sights high enough, and who knows what you might accomplish!

Let's practice. Suppose you held one of the jobs listed below. What could you do to make a difference in the lives of American families if you were:

- Your boss?
- Principal of your school?
- Superintendent of your school district?
- Mayor of your city?
- Secretary of Education?
- Secretary of Health and Human Services?
- Secretary of Agriculture?
- A religious leader in your faith?
- A corporate executive?
- A state legislator?
- A U.S. Senator?
- President of the United States?

Choose one position of authority and describe below what you might do.

_____
_____
_____
_____
_____
_____
_____
_____
_____
_____
_____
_____
_____
_____
_____
_____

If you could make a difference, would it be worth the effort to work toward one of these jobs.?

The price of greatness is responsibility.
—Winston Churchill

The trick is to think beyond the obvious. Stretch your imagination. Sometimes we limit our expectations. This can have unfortunate financial consequences for our families. And it can also keep you from having the kind of impact you could have, and from fulfilling the kinds of promises you might wish to make to your children and to posterity. If you are willing to take on the additional responsibility and commitment that go with authority and power, you can accomplish a great deal. Not just for yourself, but for everyone.

Let's look at some examples. Perhaps you think you could be a good teacher's aide. In that position, you might have some influence over one or two students, but you won't have much authority, as a rule. If you become a teacher, you might have a greater influence on children and, perhaps, their parents. Now, suppose you become a school principal. In that position, you could have something to say about how all the teachers conduct their classes. You might well influence dozens of young lives. If that principal were to go on and become the superintendent of schools, you might be responsible for encouraging hundreds of students to go after their dreams.

In a similar way, as a nurse's aide you would have little influence on your patients or your hospital. A nurse would have more power, a medical technician possibly still more, and a physician could do a great deal to affect the operation of their hospital and the lives of their patients.

Now it's your turn. Suppose you had the entry-level jobs listed below. Use your imagination to determine what course you might take to lead you to a position of greater authority and power. What might you do if you were a:

Store clerk?   ⇨ _Department Manager_ ⇨ _Store Manager_   ⇨ _Store Owner_

Child care worker?   ⇨ _____ ⇨ _____ ⇨ _____

Receptionist?   ⇨ _____ ⇨ _____ ⇨ _____

Legal secretary?   ⇨ _____ ⇨ _____ ⇨ _____

Newspaper reporter? ⇨ _____ ⇨ _____ ⇨ _____

What are the keys to advancing within a career? (Hint: Turn back to pages 126 to 153 for review.)

_____

_____

The Changing Workplace

Simply by increasing their numbers in the world of work, women have had an influence on the way business is conducted. That trend can only continue. As women have an increasing amount of power over what goes on, the environment should become less and less alien to females and the kinds of values they traditionally hold. As we pointed out in Chapter 9, it should become easier for managers to treat their employees with a degree of empathy, admitting that everyone has a life outside the corporation—and that it is sometimes questionable which life should take precedence.

And it should become easier to combine career and family life, according to such trend watchers as John Naisbitt and Patricia Aburdene. In their book, *Re-inventing the Corporation*, they report that companies are beginning to change their perceptions of—and their policies on—such issues as day care, relocation, maternity and paternity leave, and rules against employing spouses. In addition, Naisbitt and Aburdene say women are having more success in getting part-time jobs or working on a contract basis in their careers while they have young children.[2]

The success is due, in part, to the *number* of women now in the workforce. Then, too, many bosses have now had to deal with the problems of raising a family in a two-career household themselves. Today's entrepreneurs also have more creative ideas for combining success at home and on the job.

As we pointed out in Chapter 9, women are changing things by the way they relate to other people at work—not by threats and intimidation, but by empathy and intuition. In short, the workplace is becoming a better place for everyone. And you just might work yourself into a position to make further improvements. Consider what you might do about the following issues:

Comparable Worth

Comparable worth is the demand which is replacing the old cry of "equal pay for equal work." Equal pay advocates argue that, when they perform the same job, men and women should receive the same salary. And, of course, they should. This solution does not deal with one important aspect of pay discrimination, however. As you learned in Chapter 2, job categories still tend to be somewhat sex-segregated. Most secretaries, for example, are still women. And most truck drivers are still men. And jobs held mostly by men still tend to pay more than jobs held mostly by women. Even though it takes *at least* as much skill to be a secretary as it does to drive a truck, secretaries generally make less money than do truck drivers.

People in favor of comparable worth say this shouldn't be so. They think that jobs should be categorized according to the amount of education required, the skills involved, the amount of responsibility taken and so on. And the jobs of "comparable worth" should pay about equally.

There has been strong opposition to the idea. One judge, in a ruling against comparable worth, said, "This is a case which is pregnant with the possibility of disrupting the entire economic system of the United States of America...I'm not going to restructure the entire economy of the U.S."

Other people think it makes a good deal of sense and is workable as well. In fact, it is already working in a growing number of places. State employees in Minnesota will receive $42 million over four years as part of a plan to bring the salaries of women in traditional jobs in line with those of men. In Los Angeles, 3,900 clerks and librarians, most of them female, have been granted $12 million in comparable-worth raises.[3]

Public employers and unions seem to be more serious about the issue than private corporations. To quote from *Re-inventing the Corporation*, "In the corporate mind-set, management is still a man's world. And that is why there is so much scoffing at such notions as comparable worth."[4]

Suppose you were in a position to change that. If you were the Chief Executive Officer of a corporation, what would be your position on comparable worth? Why? Make your decision and explain it in the space below.

Maternity Leave

In the past, most young mothers did not have jobs outside the home. Jobs were something that women used to occupy their time until they married. If they married well, women were not expected to ever hold a job again. So there was not much need for a federal or corporate policy on maternity leave.

Today, of course, women *do* work when they are pregnant and when they have small children. But those in political power don't seem to have noticed. Unlike all Western European countries, the United States has no federal law on maternity leave. Most big corporations make some provision for parenting, but benefits can be revoked at any time. Most women do not benefit from these leaves, anyway, since about three-fourths of them work for someone other than a major corporation.

In her book, *A Lesser Life*, Sylvia Ann Hewlett contrasts the American situation with that in other nations. Her 1981 survey of 250 large U.S. corporations showed that 88 percent offered maternity leave of some kind. The average was six weeks' paid leave plus six weeks' unpaid leave. Most of these corporations also guarantee job protection.[5]

Hewlett contrasts maternity leave in America with the situation in Sweden. There, either parent is eligible for nine months' leave at the birth of a child. Up to a specified maximum, the family receives 90 percent of its earnings during this time. In addition, there is no loss of seniority or fringe benefits, and the parent is assured of returning to the same, or a similar, job.[6]

Some employers object to the idea of holding a job open for a woman while she is on maternity leave. They claim that this makes it too difficult for them to operate their businesses. It has been pointed out, though, that these same businesses had little trouble providing the same kind of benefit to men when they returned from war.

What do you think? Should there be a law mandating maternity leave? If you were a legislator, what kind of law would you introduce or support? Or should employers be left to set up their own policies? If you were an employer, what kind of policy would you want to establish? Explain below.

Child Care

After working through the first 11 chapters of this book, you should have a fairly realistic view of the kind of child care available in this country. You should also have some thoughts about the care you would hope to provide for your own children. Review Chapters 2, 10 and 11 if you need to refresh your memory.

Now suppose you are in a position to determine child care policies for your company, or even your state or national government. What would you do to make sure that children received the best possible care? What would you do to make life easier for the parents of these children? Consider the following questions before you decide.

> Would you give everyone more vacation time so that families could spend a block of time together during the year?
>
> Would you set up an on-site day care center at your place of business?
>
> Would you pay day care workers well enough to make this an attractive career option?
>
> Would you permit parents to receive supplemental payments for day care as part of their benefit package?
>
> Would you set up public pre-schools open to the children of all *working* parents?
>
> Would you set up public pre-schools open to the children of *all* parents?
>
> Would you have a sliding scale for pre-school tuition, based on the income of the parents?
>
> Would you have public service organizations set up free day care centers run by volunteers?
>
> Would you set up day care centers in retirement homes, where older people could help care for the young?
>
> Would you give single parents or low-income families first chance at openings in day care centers?

These are just a few possibilities. Can you think of others? If you could prescribe any arrangement you wanted for parents and children, what would it be? Describe it below.

Getting Political

Twenty years ago women who were politically active on behalf of other women were called "women's libbers," "bra burners" and some less polite names best forgotten. Today it's downright respectable for a woman to be involved in politics. And there are lots of ways to do it. Whether you see yourself giving a rousing campaign speech in front of thousands of cheering supporters, or quietly explaining to your neighbor why you will not vote for the candidate who wants to cut back funding for child nutrition programs, you can make a difference. At every level, political involvement shows courage. It shows a willingness to risk other valuable things in the hope of improving the lives of all. It makes you a hero. Here are some things you might do:

VOTE.
This is the obligation and privilege of every citizen. Don't take it lightly. Early in this century, women were spat upon and pelted with eggs when they demanded the right to vote. They chained themselves to fences and they went to jail. They knew the literal and symbolic power of this simple act. Carry it on.

BE INFORMED.
You can't change things if you don't know what's going on. It's important to know the issues and have an informed opinion. Even though you are busy, take the time to read newspapers and magazines. Talk about the issues with people you respect. Often you'll gain important insights.

LET PEOPLE KNOW WHAT YOU THINK.
You don't have to carry a sign or start an argument, but a quiet comment or a simple question can sometimes lead others to rethink their position. Write letters about your concerns to people in office. Write letters to the editors of the newspapers and magazines you read.

ATTEND PUBLIC HEARINGS. BE AN ADVOCATE FOR YOUR CAUSE.
If you are well-versed on an issue, you may be able to testify before your city council or legislative committee when these groups are considering action. Even if you don't want to make a speech, your presence at these meetings can communicate to the law makers the level of concern among voters.

JOIN A POLITICAL/SOCIAL ACTION GROUP.
These can function both as political bodies and volunteer organizations. For example, they may endorse a political candidate or take a stance on a particular issue. But they may also work on a local level to set up shelters for battered women, provide services for displaced homemakers and so on. See the next section of this chapter for more information.

JOIN A POLITICAL PARTY OR GROUP.
You may choose to work within the political party of your choice, or you might join an organization such as the National Women's Political Caucus, which concentrates on women's issues and electing more women to office. For more information, see the next section of this chapter. If you want to get involved in one of the major parties, you need to find out how it operates in your state. Typically, parties hold caucuses early in election years for the purpose of electing delegates to county, district or state conventions. By attending your caucus, you can raise issues of concern, vote for delegates who share your views or become a delegate yourself. As you become more experienced or better known with this party you might become a delegate to a state or national political convention, an officer of the party or even a candidate.

WORK FOR A CANDIDATE.
If you find a political candidate you truly believe in, don't just vote—go to work for her or him! Volunteers are always needed. Activities can include everything from stuffing envelopes and making phone calls to door-to-door campaigning. With the appropriate skills and experience, you might even become a paid staff member. In that capacity, you might become involved in organizing campaign events, writing speeches, handling publicity or raising money.

MAKE YOUR COMMITMENT YOUR CAREER.
There are many opportunities for paid employment in organizations that are fundamentally involved in public welfare or political change. You might choose to put your leadership skills to work as head of a non-profit organization, rather than in the corporate world, for example. Or you might choose a specialty in line with your commitment within a given profession. Instead of being a plastic surgeon, you might want to work with terminally-ill children. You might want to work in a legal aid clinic rather than in a corporate law firm.

BECOME A PROFESSIONAL ORGANIZER OR LOBBYIST.
With knowledge, experience and dedication to a cause, you might get a job as, perhaps, a union organizer among clerical workers or a lobbyist for comparable worth. You need to be an extremely persuasive person to hold jobs like these. Hours can be long and grueling, but it can be rewarding, as well.

WORK FOR AN OFFICE HOLDER.
Every office holder, from your city council representative to the President of the United States, has a staff. These people work behind the scenes, but often have a great deal of influence over what issues are addressed and what tasks are accomplished. Again, though, you need to be a committed and educated person, perhaps with a background in economics, social science, government or law, if you want to be hired.

RUN FOR OFFICE.
More women are running for office than ever before. And many of them have been elected. In 1984, there were 1,067 women serving in state legislatures. Women are, or have been, the mayors of major cities, including San Francisco, Chicago and Houston. And, as they gain experience and recognition on state and local levels, women will become more prominent on the national political scene. In the November, 1986 election, one woman was elected to the U.S. Senate, while another lost her bid for re-election. There are still only two female senators. There's a long way to go!

Getting Involved

There are dozens of ways to get involved as a political activist, community volunteer or advocate for your cause, no matter who you are or where you live. Women and men have been volunteering their time to improve the lives of others for many years. Time to spare is now a limited item for most people but, unfortunately, there is no shortage of problems to solve or people to help. Do try to get involved.

Keep in mind that volunteer work does not have to be as consistent a part of your life as your paid job. Many women find that there are times in their lives when volunteering fits in nicely, and other times when it just doesn't fit in at all. You might be quite active within an organization before the birth of your children, for example. With a baby to care for, you might have to cut back or give up your volunteer work for a period of years.

On the other hand, many volunteers today are women who have temporarily given up paid employment to care for their young children. They find the work stimulating and satisfying, and appreciate the opportunity to use their skills—or gain new ones. In addition, they might find the experience they gain, or the people they meet, valuable for their careers when they return to paid employment.

Here are the names and addresses of some organizations that work for the benefit of women and children. Keep in mind that there are, literally, thousands of local, state, national and international organizations looking for members. In addition to groups dealing specifically with women's issues, you might be interested in working for causes affecting us all, including peace, justice, the environment, hunger and poverty.

Alpha Kappa Alpha
5211 South Greenwood Avenue
Chicago, IL 60615

Altrusa
Eight South Michigan Avenue
Chicago, IL 60603

American Association of University Women
2401 Virginia Avenue, NW
Washington, DC 20037

American Business Women's Association
9100 Ward Parkway
Kansas City, MO 64114

Americans For Indian Opportunity
1010 Massachusetts Avenue NW, Suite 200
Washington, DC 20036

Association of Junior Leagues, Inc.
825 Third Avenue
New York, NY 10022

B'nai B'rith Women
1640 Rhode Island Avenue NW
Washington, DC 20036

Child Care Action Campaign
99 Hudson Street, Room 1233
New York, NY 10013

Church Women United
475 Riverside Drive, Room 812
New York, NY 10115

Delta Kappa Gamma Society International
P.O. Box 1589
Austin, TX 78767

Delta Sigma Theta Sorority, Inc.
1707 New Hampshire Avenue NW
Washington, DC 20009

Displaced Homemakers Network
1010 Vermont Ave. NW, Suite 817
Washington, DC 20005

General Federation of Women's Clubs
1734 N St. NW
Washington, DC 20036

Girls Clubs of America, Inc.
205 Lexington Avenue
New York, NY 10016

Girl Scouts of the U.S.A.
830 Third Avenue
New York, NY 10022

The League of Women Voters
1730 M St. N.W.
Washington, DC 20036

Mexican American Women's National Association
1201 16th Street NW, Room 420
Washington, DC 20036

The National Women's Political Caucus
1275 K St. NW, Suite 750
Washington, DC 20005

National Association for Female Executives
120 East 56th Street
New York, NY 10022

National Association of Commissions for Women
336 Northfield Avenue
West Orange, NJ 07052

National Council of Negro Women
701 North Fairfax Street, Suite 330
Alexandria, VA 22314

National Committee on Pay Equity
1201 16th Street NW, Room 422
Washington, DC 20036

National Council of Jewish Women
15 East 26th Street
New York, NY 10010

National Federation of Business
  and Professional Women
2012 Massachusetts Ave. NW
Washington, DC 20036

The National Organization for Women
1401 New York Ave. NW, Suite 800
Washington, DC 20005

9 to 5, National Association of
  Working Women
1224 Huron Road
Cleveland, OH 44115

Pioneer Women
200 Madison Avenue
New York, NY 10016

Women's Action Alliance
370 Lexington Ave.
New York, NY 10017

Women's Campaign Fund
815 15th St. NW, Suite 601
Washington, DC 20005

Women's Legal Defense Fund
2000 P St. NW
Washington, DC 20036

Young Women's Christian Association of the U.S.A.
726 Broadway
New York, NY 10020

Zonta International
35 East Wacker Drive
Chicago, IL 60601

Your Money or Your Time

What can you do if you just *do not* have the time to get involved in politics or community affairs? Do what so many men do: Support your favorite causes financially. It takes a great deal of money today to get things done. Elections, in particular, often go to the candidate who has the most financial support. Women are just beginning to make the kind of money needed to give the people and issues they support the financial backing men have been quietly providing to their candidates and causes for years.

If you are rich enough, you might even set up a foundation to bestow money on projects you think are worthwhile. If you don't have your own private fortune to give away, but you like the idea, you might think about going to work for someone else's foundation.

However you choose to do it, it's important to give something back. It's important to society and it's an important part of a full and successful life. Add a cause you believe in to a job you are good at, and a family you love and you get: more choices, more rewards, so many possibilities!

Lifelong Planning

Though most of this book has been about planning for the years when you are likely to have children living at home, those years will probably take up just a fraction of your adult life. Turn back to the exercise on page 21 to review how many years you might have to concentrate on other things.

It's not too soon to start considering what those other things might be. Would you like to change careers? Devote time to your favorite political or charitable organization? Have more time for friends or for yourself? Take up a new hobby?

There is a whole world full of things to do—and things that need to be done. The happiest people seem to be those who make time for themselves *and* for commitments in the outside world. In the end, your family includes more than your spouse and your children. It extends to embrace people everywhere.

What do you think you might like to do? Write your ideas below. Even if you change your mind, you will find it interesting to look back on these statements in the future. They may show you how much you've changed. Or, if you've lost sight of your goals somewhere along the way, this list could help you recover a lost dream.

"It doesn't matter where you come from as long as you know where you're going."

We hope that, by this time, you have a good idea of where *you* would like to go. One of the most important choices you will ever make is the choice to go after the life you want to lead. Hold on to your dream, believe in it and work to make it come true. No one can do it for you. No one can hold you back.

A journey of a thousand leagues begins with a single step.

—Lao-tzu

Secret of the Sea

Come, restive soul
Who beats against
The walls of circumstance,
And seeks to find
A better way, and can't—
Reach out for solace to the sea,
Undaunted through eternity.
Her ceaseless rhythms
Sing to thee
The song of those
Who would be free:

The shore does not
Confine the sea.
The sea defines the shore.

William P. Sheehan

©1986 William P. Sheehan
Reprinted with permission

Index

Affirmations 133, 140
Attitude 126, 141-43, 148-51
Balance 156-69, 167, 217
Budget 42-46, 195-96
Careers 68-77, 80-82, 101, 103, 116, 120-21, 143, 157, 199, 201, 210-13
   non-traditional 116
   professional 80-82
   traditional 116
Child Care 31-32, 177, 193-96, 228-29
Commitment 130-31, 146, 148
Communication Skills 152
Competence 128-29, 148, 150
Confidence 132-33, 148, 150
Consultant 88-89
Control 127, 146-51, 160, 198-99
   5 Cs of 127, 146-51, 160

Courage 137-39, 149, 151
Creativity 134-36, 149, 151
Divorce 35-36
Education 118-19, 153
   vocational 118-19
Entrepreneur 93-98
Flexibility 77, 81-82, 87-88, 101, 118, 121-22
Free-lancer 83-85
Health 161-62
Housework 178-81
Income, dual 176-77, 182
Jobs 101-03, 120-21
Ladder, career 199, 213
Leave, maternity 227-28
Manager 90-92
Math 140-48
Money 42, 47-56, 58-61, 68, 234

Motherhood 20-21
Myth 8-23, 26, 182
Needs, financial 208-09
Parent 28-34, 67, 72, 158, 192, 197, 200
   single 28-34, 67
   working 197
Planning 39, 193, 204-06, 235
Poverty, feminization of 35-36
Power 222
Priorities 156, 163-68
Reality 29-38
Relationships 157, 174-75, 177, 187-89
Salaries 68-70, 74-75, 118-19, 121
Sales Person 86-87
Self-sufficiency 16

Statistics
   average annual salaries 74
   average hourly salaries 68
   child care 31-32, 193
   entrepreneurs 93
   part-time workforce 80
   poverty and divorce 35
   wage gap 107
   working woman 29-30
Stress 160, 197-98
Superwoman 22, 27, 169
Technology 100-101
Time 65-71
Traits 182-86
Values
   career 57
Wage gap 107-110
Wonderwoman 169-70
Worth, comparable 226

Contributors

The authors wish to give special recognition to the following peer reviewers and consultants whose suggestions and contributions helped to make this book what it is. We wish to thank them for taking time out of their busy schedules to read manuscripts and share their expertise and ideas.

Elaine Reuben, Ph.D., organization consultant, speaker, trainer (Washington, D.C.)

Jim Comiskey, lecturer and author of *How to Start, Expand and Sell a Business, The Complete Guidebook for Entrepreneurs*

Anna Marie Hutchison, author of IRA *Investing Made Easy* and lecturer, "Building a Financially Secure Life," and Chair of the Board of the California Cable Television Association, 1982-83

Heather Johnston-Nicholson, Ph.D., Director of the Girls Clubs of America National Resource Center and author of *Facts and Reflections on Careers for Today's Girls* and *Facts and Reflections on Female Adolescent Sexuality*

Connie LaFace-Olson, Director, Commission for Sex Equity, Los Angeles Unified School District

Betty Stambolian, National Secretary/Treasurer, Vocational Education Equity Council and Equity Coordinator, New Jersey Department of Education

Mary Wiberg, President, National Association of Commissions for Women and Vocational Equity Consultant for the Iowa Department of Education

Dolores Wisdom, Information Specialist, Girls Clubs of America National Resource Center

More Choices curriculum evaluators: Velma Butler, Knox High School, Indiana; JoBerta Hein, C.H.E., North Posey High School, Indiana; Dr. Karen Spencer, Vocational Equity Consultant, Omaha, Nebraska.

Special thanks to Graphic Traffic for the typography.

Notes

Chapter One
1. Heather Johnston Nicholson, Ph.D., *Facts and Reflections on Careers for Today's Girls* (New York: Girls Clubs of America, Inc., 1985), p. 31.
2. John Naisbitt, *Megatrends* (New York: Warner Books, 1984), p. 82.
3. Sylvia Ann Hewlett, *A Lesser Life* (New York: Morrow, 1986), p. 23.

Chapter Two
1. American Council of Life Insurance, Community and Consumer Relations. *Factsheet on Women* (Fall 1983).
2. Ibid.
*3. Howard Hayghe, "Working Mothers Reach Record Number in 1984," *Monthly Labor Review*, 107, 12, (December 1984), pp. 31-34.
4. Bureau of Labor Statistics, "Employment Projections for 1995", BLS Bull., 2197, (March 1984).
*5. Bureau of Labor Statistics, U.S. Department of Labor, *Employment and Earnings* (July 1984), 31:7.
*6. U.S. Department of Labor, Office of the Secretary, Women's Bureau. 20 Facts on Women's Workers, (1984).
*7. Janet L. Norwood, "Introduction", *The Female-Male Earnings Gap: A Review of Employment and Earnings Issues.* (Washington D.C., U.S. Department of Labor, Bureau of Labor Statistics, Sept. 1982).
*8. *20 Facts on Women Workers*.
*9. Peter Francese, "People Patterns", *The Indianapolis Star*, 22 July 1984.
10. Telephone communication with the Bureau of Labor Statistics, United States Department of Labor and the Census Bureau, United States Department of Commerce, 1985.
11. Hewlett, *A Lesser Life*, p. 23.
12. *Corporations and Two Career Families: Directions for the Future* (New York: Catalyst Career and Family Center, 1981) 15-16.
13. Hewlett, *A Lesser Life*, p. 119.
14. Bureau of Labor Statistics, "Women at Work: A Chartbook," BLS Bulletin 2197, (March 1984).
15. Hewlett, *A Lesser Life*, p. 109.
16. Ibid., p. 118.
17. Ibid., p. 120.
18. Ibid., p. 124.
19. Ibid., p. 109.
20. *Monthly Labor Review* (December 1983), 18.
21. Hewlett, *A Lesser Life*, p. 66.
22. Lenore J. Weitzman, "The Economics of Divorce: Social and Economic Consequences of Property, Alimony and Child Support Awards," UCLA Law Review 28 (August 1981), 1266.
23. Ibid.
24. Hewlett, *A Lesser Life*, p. 69.
25. Ibid., p. 62.
26. Ibid., p. 60.
27. Ibid., p. 14.
28. Ibid., p. 71.
29. Ibid., pp. 91-92.

Chapter Four
1. Marjorie Hansen Shaevitz, *The Superwoman Syndrome* (New York: Warner Books, Inc., 1984), p. 93.

Chapter Five
1. Women's Bureau, U.S. Department of Labor, *Time of Change: 1983 Handbook on Women Workers* (Washington, D.C.: U.S. Department of Labor, 1983).

Chapter Six
1. *Money, Income and Poverty Status of Families and Persons in the U.S.: 1984*, Current Population Reports, Series P-60 (Washington, D.C.: Bureau of the Census, August 1985), p. 17.
*2. Elizabeth Waldman, "Today's Girls in Tomorrow's Labor Force: Projecting Their Participation and Occupations," *Youth and Society* (March 1985), pp. 375-392.
*3. *20 Facts on Women's Workers*.
*4. *Time of Change: 1983 Handbook on Women Workers*.
5. Ellen Wojohn, "Why Aren't There More Women In This Magazine?" INC. July 1986, p. 49.
6. Ibid., p. 49.
7. Hewlett, *A Lesser Life*, p. 71.
8. Ibid.
9. Ibid., p. 116.
10. Ibid., p. 74.

Chapter Seven
1. Naisbitt, *Megatrends*, p. 7.

Chapter Ten
1. Current Population Reports, *Child Care Arrangements of Working Mothers*, Series P-23 (Washington, D.C.: U.S. Bureau of the Census, 1983), p. 22.

Chapter Twelve
1. Thomas R. Dye and Julie Strickland, "Women at the Top: A Note on Institutional Leadership," *Social Science Quarterly* 63,2 (June 1982), pp. 333-341.
2. John Naisbitt and Patricia Aburdene, *Re-inventing the Corporation* (New York: Warner Books, 1985), p. 238.
3. Ibid., pp. 260-261.
4. Ibid., p. 264.
5. Hewlett, *A Lesser Life*, p. 93.
6. Ibid., p. 96.

* As cited in *Facts and Reflections on Careers for Today's Girls*, by Heather Johnston Nicholson, Ph.D, (New York: Girls Clubs of America, 1985)

ILLUSTRATIONS

Alma Barkley — pages 26, 28, 37, 39, 106, 108, 110, 112-113, 114, 116, 117, 118, 120, 121, 123, 137, 156, 163, 168, 169, 201.

Janice Blair — pages 2, 8-9, 10, 11, 16, 33, 34, 47, 49, 50-51, 52, 53, 54, 55, 56, 64-65, 67, 76, 77, 80, 82, 85, 86, 97, 99, 100, 102, 103, 139, 140, 144, 148, 150, 174, 175, 176, 177, 183, 184, 187, 189, 192, 194, 197, 199, 228, 240.

Dorie Hutchinson — pages 14, 20, 31, 32, 128, 178, 207, 210, 212, 220-221.

Itoko Maeno — pages 1, 4-5, 6-7, 12-13, 19, 22, 23, 24-25, 27, 40-41, 42-43, 44-45, 46, 59, 61, 62-63, 68, 69, 72, 74, 78-79, 88, 89, 90, 93, 94, 98, 104-105, 124-125, 126-127, 130, 131, 132, 134, 135, 143, 146, 147, 152-153, 154-155, 160, 161, 162, 165, 166, 167, 171, 172-173, 181, 190-191, 193, 195, 202-203, 214, 218-219, 222, 225, 230, 233, 234, 236-237.

Laurie Whitfield — pages 83, 204-205, 208, 216-217.

Art Director — Itoko Maeno

Other books by Advocacy Press:

Choices: A Teen Woman's Journal for Self-awareness and Personal Planning, by Mindy Bingham, Judy Edmondson and Sandy Stryker. Softcover, 240 pages. ISBN 0-911655-22-0.

Challenges: A Young Man's Journal for Self-awareness and Personal Planning, by Bingham, Edmondson and Stryker. Softcover, 240 pages. ISBN 0-911655-24-7.

Gifts every parent, grandparent and caring adult will want to give the teenagers in their lives. CHOICES and CHALLENGES seriously address the myths and hard realities each sex faces in today's changing world. They contain thought-provoking [...] about their futures, develop quantitative [...], and evaluate career options, [...] budgeting.

Changes: A [...] ***Planning,*** by Bingham, Stryker, and [...] 40-9. By popular demand, our best-selling [...] women.

Minou, by M[...] over with dust jacket, lovely full-col[...] ISBN 0-911655-36-0.

This cha[...] introduces a life concept still, regr[...] — the reality that everyone, especially [...] themselves. It is everything a children's [...] meaningful.

Father Gand[...] [...] by Father Gander. Hardcover wi[...] 48 pages, ISBN 0-91165[...]

Without [...] original *Mother Goose* rhymes, each of F[...] positive message in which both sexes, all [...] handicaps interact naturally and successfu[...]

You can find these books at better bookstores. Or you may order them directly by sending $14.45 each (includes shipping) to Advocacy Press, P.O. Box 236, Dept. A, Santa Barbara, California 93102. For your review we will be happy to send you more information on these publications.